W9-CJC-310

PUBLIC LIBRARY DISTRICT OF COLUMBIA

STECK-VAUGHN

Vocabulary Advantage

FOR

Life Science and Biology

Student Work Text

Vivian Bernstein

Steck Vaughn™

A Harcourt Achieve Imprint

www.Steck-Vaughn.com
1-800-531-5015

Reading Level:	**8 - 10**
Category:	**Instructional - Language**
Subcategory:	**Vocabulary/Skill Building**
Workbook Available:	
Teacher Guide Available:	**Yes**
Part of a Series:	**Yes**
CD / CD ROM / DVD Available:	

HAGLO LIBRARY DISTRICT OF CLO...

Acknowledgements

Executive Editor   Eduardo Aparicio
Senior Editor   Victoria Davis
Design Team   Cindi Ellis, Cynthia Hannon,
                            Jean O'Dette

Media Researchers   Nicole Mlakar, Stephanie Arsenault
Production Team   Mychael Ferris-Pacheco,
                            Paula Schumann, Alia Hasan

Creative Team   Joan Cunningham, Alan Klemp

Photo Credits

Page 20d ©NIBSC/Photo Researchers, Inc.; p. 22d ©Dr. Gopal Murti/Photo Researchers, Inc.;
p. 32d ©USDA/Nature Source/Photo Researchers, Inc.; p. 38d ©Bettmann/CORBIS; p. 44d
©Mark Moffett/Minden Pictures; p. 62d ©Greg Latza/AP Photo; p. 68d ©David Arky/CORBIS;
p. 74d ©OSF/Animals Animals-Earth Scenes.

Additional photography by Artville/Getty Images Royalty Free, Comstock Royalty Free, Digital
Vision/Getty Images Royalty Free, Dynamic Graphics/Liquid Library, PhotoDisc/Getty Images Royalty Free, Photos.com Royalty Free, and Royalty-Free/CORBIS.

ISBN 1-4190-1890-6

© 2007 Harcourt Achieve Inc.

All rights reserved. No part of the material protected by this copyright may be reproduced
or utilized in any form or by any means, in whole or in part, without permission in writing
from the copyright owner. Requests for permission should be mailed to: Paralegal
Department, 6277 Sea Harbor Drive, Orlando, FL 32887

Steck-Vaughn is a trademark of Harcourt Achieve Inc.

Printed in the United States of America
1 2 3 4 5 6 7 8 082 12 11 10 09 08 07 06 05

Dear Student,

Welcome to *Vocabulary Advantage for Life Science and Biology*!

In this Student Work Text, you will

- learn new life science and biology words that will help you better understand what you read in your life science and biology textbook,

- learn useful words that will help you in the classroom and on tests, and

- learn skills that will help you figure out the meaning of other new words.

You will write and talk about the new words you've learned. You should also feel free to draw, circle, underline, and make notes on the pages of this Work Text to help you remember what the new words mean. You can do more writing and drawing in your Life Science and Biology Vocabulary Journal.

At the end of this book, you will find a glossary and a list of test-taking tips.

All of the tools in this book will help you build your own understanding of important biology and classroom vocabulary. Building your understanding of these words will give you an advantage in your life science and biology class and on life science and biology tests!

Have fun!

Table of Contents

Lesson 1 Science Tools

Read the passage below. Think about the meanings of the new words in **bold**. Underline any definitions that might help you figure out what the new words mean. The first one has been done for you.

Thinking Science

Vocabulary Strategy

Writers will often include definitions of new or difficult words near those words in the text. Look for these definitions to help you understand the meanings of new words.

There are many kinds of scientists. Astronomers study the stars and outer space. Botanists study plants. Chemists and physicists study the materials that make up the earth. Even though they may study very different things, these people all *think* like scientists. Scientists constantly ask questions and try to gather **data**, <u>information that they can study to help them answer their questions.</u>

There are three ways that scientists gather and use data. **Observation** involves observing or carefully watching something in order to gain information. An **investigation** is an organized way of gathering information. The ways individual scientists observe and investigate may be very different, however. One scientist might work with computers in a lab, while another might search through a rain forest for undiscovered plants.

Once they make new discoveries, scientists attempt to classify what they've found out. **Classification** is the grouping together of similar kinds of information.

So, you should start thinking like a scientist if you want to be a scientist someday!

New Life Science and Biology Words

classification

    noun   a way of grouping things based on their similarities

data

    noun   information, facts, or numbers gathered for a purpose

investigation

    noun   an organized plan for gathering information about something

observation

    noun   the act of carefully watching something to gather information about it

Now read this passage and practice the vocabulary strategy again. Underline any definitions in the passage that can help you figure out what the new words in **bold** mean.

The Scientific Method

The scientific method was developed during the Age of Reason, from around 1600 to 1700. Scientists at this time set up experiments and carefully observed the results. They followed a **process**, or series of actions that helped them get to the same result time after time. They set up experiments in which everything would be the same except for one **variable**, or the thing being tested. They made **predictions**, or guesses about what would happen if they changed the variables. They asked questions about everything.

Benjamin Franklin's famous kite experiment is an example of the scientific method. Franklin made a **hypothesis**, or a guess, that lightning was electricity in the air. He tested his hypothesis by attaching an iron key to a kite string. While his son flew the kite into storm clouds, Franklin held his hand up to the key and watched a spark jump from the key to his knuckle. Based on the facts he gathered, Franklin stated his **theory** about lightning. Lightning could be **defined**, or explained as electricity.

More New Life Science and Biology Words

hypothesis

   noun   a guess or an idea that can be tested

process

   noun   a series of a events or actions that produce a result

theory

   noun   a statement, based on facts, that explains why or how something happens

variable

   noun the thing that is tested in an experiment
   adjective   able to change

"My **hypothesis** is that Jason didn't get enough sleep last night."

Other Useful Words

define

   verb   to describe or explain something completely

predict

   verb   to guess what will happen

Apply the Strategy

Look at a chapter in your textbook that your teacher identifies. Use definitions in the text to help you figure out the meaning of any new words you find.

Extend the Meaning

Write the letter of the word or phrase that best completes each sentence. Discuss your choices with a partner.

1 A **theory** might _____.
    a. show how to do an experiment
    b. explain why flowers are certain colors
    c. tell the number of people living in a city

2 A **classification** might include _____.
    a. the amount of rainfall for each month of a year
    b. a drawing of a leaf
    c. plants or animals that have something in common

3 You can use **data** to _____.
    a. create a graph or table
    b. show how to pour acid into a test tube
    c. demonstrate how snakes lay eggs

4 When you **define** a word, you _____.
    a. spell it
    b. explain what it means
    c. tell how it should be said

5 A person might perform an **investigation** to _____.
    a. gather information
    b. draw a diagram
    c. catch a salamander

6 A **variable** is _____.
    a. something that can be changed
    b. something that can never change
    c. something that is not very useful

7 A **process** might _____.
    a. explain why something is made
    b. describe the life cycle of an animal
    c. follow the steps of a recipe to make a cake

8 A **hypothesis** is _____.
    a. always correct
    b. a guess based on facts
    c. almost never correct

9 An **observation** might _____.
    a. describe the color of a certain kind of flower
    b. explain how plants make food
    c. be a kind of prediction

10 When you **predict**, you _____.
    a. explain what something is
    b. guess what might happen next
    c. test an idea

Word Challenge: Correct or Incorrect

Take turns with a partner reading the sentences below out loud. Write **C** if the sentence is correct, and write **I** if the sentence is incorrect. Rewrite the incorrect sentences. The first one has been done for you.

1 ___C__ We put all of the **data** we gathered into a graph to help us analyze our results.

2 _____ The animals in that **classification** had nothing in common.

_____

3 _____ Our teacher told us that a good **investigation** has no order to it.

_____

4 _____ During our **observation**, the plant's leaves turned from green to brown.

_____

5 _____ I **define** scientist s-c-i-e-n-t-i-s-t.

_____

Word Challenge: Which Word?

With a partner, take turns saying the words listed below. Together, think of a statement for each one that gives a strong clue about its meaning. Write your statement next to the word. The first one has been done for you.

1 **hypothesis** _"I'm an idea that can be tested."_

2 **process** _____

3 **variable** _____

4 **predict** _____

5 **theory** _____

The Right Word

Read each sentence. Look at the word or phrase that is underlined. Write one of the words from the box that means the same or almost the same thing as the underlined part of the sentence. Discuss your answers with a partner.

classification	data	observation	theory	variable

1 _____ Mom didn't like my <u>explanation</u> that a messy room helps me study.

2 _____ We gathered <u>information and numbers</u> about the life of moths.

3 _____ The only <u>thing that could change</u> in our experiment was the type of soil.

4 _____ Plants that have flowers belong to the <u>category</u> angiosperm.

5 _____ After <u>looking at something carefully</u>, we didn't see any changes.

Word Study: The Suffixes *-able* and *-ible*

When the suffix *-able* or *-ible* is added to a root verb such as *predict,* it does two things:

- First, it makes the verb an adjective: *predictable*.
- Second, it changes the word's meaning. The word now describes something that can be predicted.

Drop the *-e* from the end of a word before adding *-able* or *-ible*.

Change the *-y* at the end of a word to *-i* before adding *-able* or *-ible*.

A. Write each word's root verb and add a suffix. Use a dictionary to check your spelling.

	Root Verb	+ *-able* or *-ible*
1 classification		
2 observation		
3 definition		

B. Complete each sentence with an adjective from the chart.

1 Something we can classify, or sort into groups is _____.

2 We could watch the clouds change. The change was _____.

3 It was easy to explain what that word meant. It was _____.

6

The Language of Testing

How would you answer a question like this on a test?

Which of the following scientists discovered how plants pass on characteristics to their offspring?

    A. Albert Einstein
    B. Gregor Mendel
    C. Marie Curie
    D. Charles Darwin

 Tip

The phrase *which of the following* means that you have to choose one of the answers (A, B, C, or D) to answer the question.

Test Strategy: Read the entire question carefully. Make sure you understand what is being asked. Then, if the question has the phrase *which of the following* in it, you may want to ask the question in a different way. Start your restated question with who, where, or what.

1 How could you say the question above in a different way?

_____

_____

Try the strategy again by asking these questions in a different way.

2 Which of the following is part of the scientific method?

    A. testing a hypothesis
    B. following a plan
    C. creating a table
    D. gathering data

3 Which of the following is where plants make much of their food?

    A. root
    B. stem
    C. seed
    D. leaf

_____   _____

_____   _____

_____   _____

In Your Vocabulary Journal

Find each of these words in your Life Science and Biology Vocabulary Journal. Working by yourself or with a partner, use the definitions from pages 2 and 3 of your Work Text to complete the rest of the entry for each word.

classification	**data**	**define**	**hypothesis**	**investigation**
observation	**predict**	**process**	**theory**	**variable**

Lesson 2 Classifying Life

Read the passage below. Think about the meanings of the new words in **bold**. Create associations between familiar words and the new words. These will help you remember what the new words mean. Mark or write these associations near the new words in the passage.

Classification

Vocabulary Strategy

Create associations between things you know and the new words to "anchor" your understanding of the new words. You can complete a Word Anchor chart to help you make associations.

You can use word games to help you remember information. For example, many students learn to spell *arithmetic* by remembering "A rat in the house might eat the ice cream." The first letters of the words in the sentence spell *arithmetic*.

There is also a way you can remember the seven levels of scientific **taxonomy**, or classification. The levels are: **kingdom**, phylum, class, **order**, family, genus, and **species**. The kingdom level is the broadest level. In it are large groups of **organisms** such as plants or animals.

a way of sorting

As the levels become narrower, the organisms become more clearly defined. The organisms in the lower levels are also more like each other than those in the top level. For example, a frog and a dog both belong to the animal kingdom. However, a dog belongs to the class mammal, and a frog belongs to the class amphibian.

Don't think you can remember the levels in order? Just think, "**K**ings **P**lay **C**hess **O**n **F**unny **G**reen **S**quares."

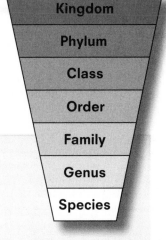

New Life Science and Biology Words

kingdom
noun   the top level of scientific classification

order
noun   the way things are placed or organized, or a level of scientific classification

organism
noun   a plant, animal, or single-celled life form

species
noun   the lowest level of scientific classification

taxonomy
noun   the classification of things, especially living organisms

Now read this passage and practice the vocabulary strategy again. Write near the new words or mark in the text any associations you can use to anchor the meaning of the new words.

Living Things

All organisms have several things in common. First, they need food and water to stay alive. If you do not water a plant, it will die. If you don't eat, you will starve. All organisms also have ways of turning food into energy. This is called **metabolism**.

Another thing that all organisms have in common is that they **respond** to light, sound, hunger, temperature, and hundreds of other things. Each of these things is a **stimulus**. Plants bend toward the light. You feel pain if you get a splinter. A lion is hungry, so it hunts for food. Organisms also need to be able to **distinguish** one stimulus from another.

They need to be able to tell the difference between hunger, thirst, pain, and so on to know what they need.

A third thing that all organisms have in common is that they can keep a balance inside their bodies. This balance is called **homeostasis**. For example, cold-blooded animals move into the sunlight to keep their body temperature warm enough. Some plants have thick skins to keep them from losing moisture. Some frogs even bury themselves deep in the ground during dry periods in order to stay alive.

More New Life Science and Biology Words

homeostasis

noun   the balance that living things keep in their bodies

metabolism

noun   the way a living thing changes food into energy

stimulus

noun   something that causes a reaction

"The subject is **responding** to the **stimulus** . . ."

Other Useful Words

distinguish

verb   to be able to tell the difference between or among two or more things

respond

verb   to answer or react to something

Apply the Strategy

Look at a chapter in your textbook that your teacher identifies. Create associations to help you anchor your understanding of any new words you find.

Finish the Sentence

Use a word from the box to finish each sentence. Write the correct word on the line. Discuss your choices with a partner.

homeostasis	kingdom	metabolism	organism	species

1 The plant _____ includes all plants.

2 Cold-blooded animals such as reptiles lie in the sun to keep a balance, or _____ in their body temperature.

3 Living things change food to energy through _____.

4 The lowest level of scientific classification is _____.

5 Each living thing is a(n) _____.

distinguish	respond	order	taxonomy	stimulus

6 You can _____ between an apple and an orange by taste, touch, and smell.

7 We learned scientific _____ by sorting, or classifying plants and animals.

8 How do you react, or _____, to loud noises?

9 A cheeseburger is a _____ that makes my mouth water!

10 The scientific classification that comes between *class* and *family* is _____.

Word Challenge: Finish the Idea

With a partner, take turns reading the incomplete sentences below. Write an ending for each. The first one has been done for you.

1. My body would be in a state of **homeostasis** if _I kept myself at the same temperature all the time._

2. My alarm clock is a **stimulus** because _____

_____

3. When I eat, my **metabolism** helps _____

_____

4. I can **distinguish** between being tired and being hungry because _____

_____

Word Challenge: What's Your Answer?

Take turns with a partner reading each question out loud and writing an answer on the line. Answer the questions in complete sentences. The first one has been done for you.

1. What **kingdom** do you belong to? _I belong to the animal kingdom._

2. What would a **taxonomy** of your school be like? _____

_____

3. Is your locker in **order**? Describe it. _____

_____

4. How would you **respond** if your classroom suddenly became very hot?

_____

Analogies

Use a word from the box to finish each sentence. Write the word on the line. Discuss your answers with a partner.

stimulus	metabolism	species	respond	taxonomy

1 School is to classroom as kingdom is to _____.

2 Cause is to effect as _____ is to response.

3 See is to observe as _____ is to answer.

4 Wood is to a fire as food is to _____.

5 Letters are to alphabet as creatures are to _____.

Word Study: The Prefixes *sub-* and *super-*

When a prefix *sub-* or *super-* is added to a noun, it changes the noun's meaning.
- *Sub-* adds the meaning *under* or *below*.
- *Super-* adds the meaning *over* or *above*.

> **order** (n.) the way things are arranged or organized, or a level of scientific classification
> **suborder** (n.) a level of classification that is lower than an order

A. Add *sub-* and *super-* to the following words.

	+ *sub-*	+ *super-*
1 kingdom		
2 order		
3 species		

B. Fill each blank with a *sub-* word or a *super-* word from the chart.

1 A certain species of goose lives in Canada. There are two groups, or _____ under that species.

2 There are living things that move and eat like animals, but they are not animals. They belong in a group above the animal kingdom, or a _____.

The Language of Testing

How would you answer a question like this on a test?

All of the following are levels of scientific taxonomy **except**

    A. kingdom
    B. species
    C. homeostasis
    D. order

 Tip

The word *except* in a test question means that you should look for the answer choice that is not like the other answers. You might also look for the answer that is the opposite of the others.

Test Strategy: If the question has the word *except* in it, ask the question in a different way. Use words such as *not* or *opposite*, and phrases such as *which of these answers is not like the other answers?*

1 How could you write the question above in a different way?

_____

_____

Try the strategy again by asking these questions in a different way.

2 Each of the following is a cellular function except

    A. metabolism
    B. homeostasis
    C. mitosis
    D. organelle

3 All of the following are animal species except

    A. *Ambrystoma californiense*
    B. *Rana muscosa*
    C. *Synthiliboramphus hypoleucus*
    D. *Eriastrum hooveri*

_____   _____

_____   _____

_____   _____

 In Your Vocabulary Journal

Find each of these words in your Life Science and Biology Vocabulary Journal. Working by yourself or with a partner, use the definitions from pages 8 and 9 of your Work Text to complete the rest of the entry for each word.

distinguish	**homeostasis**	**kingdom**	**metabolism**	**order**
organism	**respond**	**species**	**stimulus**	**taxonomy**

Lesson 3
Cells, the Building Blocks of Life

Read the passage below. Think about the meanings of the new words printed in **bold**. Underline any examples or descriptions you find that might help you figure out the meaning of new words. Then draw an arrow from each example or the description to the word it describes. The first one has been done for you.

The Parts of a Cell

Vocabulary Strategy

Sometimes writers use examples and descriptions to explain hard ideas or words. Look for clues like *for example*, *like*, or *such as*. Look for pictures that might explain what a new word means, too.

All organisms are made up of cells. Even though organisms can be very different, their cells are very similar. If we look at these organisms from this **cellular** level, we find that almost all cells are built the same way.

All cells have a cell **membrane**. It is a very thin, flexible skin. The cell membrane holds the contents of the cell inside. It is like a plastic zipper sandwich bag filled with water. The bag is like the cell membrane. Now, put a marble inside the bag. This is like the cell's **nucleus**. The nucleus is like the cell's brain. It controls what the cell does and how it grows. Inside the nucleus are stick-shaped **chromosomes**. The chromosomes are like a map. All of the information for what the cell does and how it will make more of itself are in the chromosomes.

No matter where cells come from, they have many things in common.

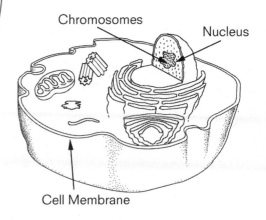

Chromosomes

Nucleus

Cell Membrane

Animal Cell

New Life Science and Biology Words

cellular

adjective   having to do with cells, the smallest unit of life

chromosome

noun   part of a cell that holds all of the cell's information

membrane

noun   the thin, outer layer of a cell or a thin, flexible skin

nucleus

noun   the central part of a cell that controls what it does

Now read this passage and practice the vocabulary strategy again. Underline the examples and descriptions in the passage. Draw an arrow from each to the new word it describes.

Special Kinds of Cells

Your body has many different kinds of cells. Each one **specializes** in something. They all have special jobs to do. Nerve cells specialize in sending messages to the brain. Muscle cells stretch and tighten. Red blood cells carry oxygen to other cells. White blood cells protect a body from disease. Some cells form **tissues**, like muscle tissue, skin tissue, lung tissue, and brain tissue.

Some specialized cells form **organs**. Your heart, lungs, and liver are all organs. Each organ does a specific job. For example, the heart pumps blood throughout the body. The lungs help oxygen enter the blood stream. They also allow carbon dioxide to escape. The stomach is where metabolism turns food into energy.

In order to function well, all types of cells need **protein**. Protein is muscle fuel. Cells can create some protein, but not enough for the whole body. That's why it is important to eat protein-rich foods like eggs, soy beans, nuts, fish, meat, and cheese.

To **conclude**, your cells do many different jobs in many different places in your body.

That's not the kind of **cellular** phone I wanted.

More New Life Science and Biology Words

organ

noun   a part of an animal that does a specific job

protein

noun   a substance that builds and keeps muscles healthy

specialize

verb   to do a specific job

tissue

noun   a large group of cells in an animal or plant that are alike and do the same job

Other Useful Words

conclude

verb   to make a final decision based on facts or observations

demonstrate

verb   to show

Apply the Strategy

Look at a chapter in your textbook that your teacher identifies. Use examples, descriptions, and pictures in the text to help you figure out the meaning of new words you find. You many want to draw pictures to help you remember what the new words mean.

Matching

Finish the sentences in Group A with words from Group B. Write the letter of the word on the line. Discuss your choices with a partner.

Group A

1 The _____ in a cell control how it will grow.

2 You need to eat foods high in _____ if you want to stay healthy.

3 Skin cells are _____. They all do a certain job.

4 You can study an organism at the _____ level only through a microscope.

5 He showed, or _____ how to make a fruit smoothie without a blender.

Group B

A. chromosomes
B. specialized
C. demonstrated
D. protein
E. cellular

Group A

6 The _____ is like a cell's brain.

7 One of your most important _____ in your body is your heart.

8 We ended, or _____, our play with a song about the Internet.

9 Your muscle _____ helps you do just about everything in your life.

10 A very thin skin, or _____, separated the two cells.

Group B

F. concluded
G. membrane
H. nucleus
I. organs
J. tissue

Word Challenge: True or False

Take turns with a partner reading the sentences below out loud. Write **T** next to each sentence that is true. Write **F** next to each sentence that is false. The first one has been done for you.

1 __T__ The brain is an **organ**.

2 _____ A **membrane** is usually very thick.

_____

3 _____ **Proteins** are necessary for your body to be strong.

_____

4 _____ The cells in a **tissue** are not alike.

_____

5 _____ You **conclude** something at the very end.

_____

Word Challenge: Would You Rather

Take turns with a partner reading the questions below out loud. Think of a response and write it on the line. Explain your answers. The first one has been done for you.

1 Would you rather **demonstrate** the importance of **protein** or just eat it?
I'd rather eat some protein because it tastes good.

2 Would you rather be a cell's **nucleus** or the **membrane**? _____
_____

3 Would you rather be an **organ** or a **tissue**? _____
_____

4 Would you rather **specialize** in sports or in art? _____
_____

Finish the Idea

Finish each idea to make a complete sentence. Write your answer on the line.

1. I like to eat **proteins** because _____

_____

2. I would describe something as **cellular** if _____

_____

3. I would like to **specialize** in _____ because _____

_____

4. A body could not survive without **tissues** because _____

_____

Word Study: The Prefixes *multi-* and *uni-*

When the prefix *multi-* is added to a noun such as *cellular*, it changes the noun's meaning.
- First, it makes the noun an adjective: *multicellular*.
- Second, it adds *many* or *more than one* to the word's meaning.

When the prefix *uni-* is added to a noun such as *cellular*, it also changes the noun's meaning.
- First, it makes the noun an adjective: *unicellular*.
- Second, it adds *one* to the word's meaning.

A. Add the *multi-* or *uni-* prefix as called for to make a new word.

		+ *multi-* or *uni-*	Meaning
1	process		more than one process
2	variable		just one variable
3	species		more than one species

B. Fill each blank with a *multi-* or *uni-* word from the chart.

1. There was one variable in the experiment. It was a _____ experiment.

2. There are many processes in this recipe. It is a _____ recipe.

18

The Language of Testing

How would you answer a question like this on a test?

What is a **characteristic** of tissue?

- A. has similar cells
- B. is found only in certain places
- C. has a variety of cells
- D. performs many functions

 Tip

A *characteristic* of a thing is something that it usually has or does.

Test Strategy: If you see a question that uses the word *characteristic*, rewrite it to ask for something that is true about the subject of the question.

1 How could you say the question above in a different way?

_____

_____

Try the strategy again by asking these questions in a different way.

2 What is a characteristic of chromosomes?

- A. They are shaped like rods.
- B. They contain tissue.
- C. They grow outside of a cell.
- D. They are similar to golgi bodies.

_____

_____

_____

3 What is a characteristic of membranes?

- A. They are not flexible.
- B. They can allow things to pass through them.
- C. They cover all organs.
- D. They give off proteins.

_____

_____

_____

In Your Vocabulary Journal

Find each of these words in your Life Science and Biology Vocabulary Journal. Working by yourself or with a partner, use the definitions from pages 14 and 15 of your Work Text to complete the rest of the entry for each word.

cellular	chromosome	conclude	demonstrate	membrane
nucleus	organ	protein	specialize	tissue

Cell Function

Read the passage below. Think about the meanings of the new words in **bold**. Underline any words or phrases that are contrasted with the new words. The first one has been done for you.

Vocabulary Strategy

Use contrasts in the text to help you understand the meanings of new words. Look for clues that point out contrasts, such as *unlike*, *instead*, or *different from*.

What Cells Do

Cells are alive, just as you are alive. In some ways, cells do the same sorts of things that you do. One of the main jobs of the cell is to take in oxygen and other substances and change them into energy. Sugars and proteins enter the cell through the membrane.

The process of moving things through a living membrane is called **transport**. Transport doesn't just mean carrying something, however. It can also mean movement. When sugars, proteins and oxygen transport into the cell, they spread out. They don't remain grouped in one area. This process is called **diffusion**.

Oxygen is needed for cells to breathe. When no oxygen is present, **fermentation** occurs. This process uses energy and releases something called lactic acid.

Another job of a cell is **replication**. This is how a cell makes new cells. It is different from reproduction, however, in that the cell doesn't join with other cells. Instead, it just splits into two. These two cells then become four, and so on.

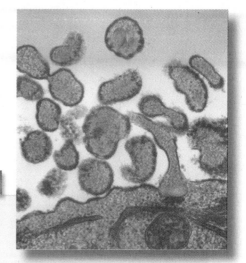

New Life Science and Biology Words

diffusion

noun   the process in which very small pieces of something move from where there are many to where there are fewer

fermentation

noun   a process that produces energy without using oxygen

replication

noun   a process in which cells make new cells

transport

verb   to move things

20

Now read this passage and practice the vocabulary strategy again. Underline any words or phrases that are contrasted with the new words in **bold**. Look for clues like *unlike*, *instead*, or *different from*.

Cell Division

Most cells divide or reproduce through a process called **mitosis**. Mitosis is different from **fission**, which is how some organisms, such as bacteria and yeast, reproduce. During mitosis, a cell splits in two, forming two cells that are exactly alike.

One of the most important **functions** of the nucleus is cell reproduction. During mitosis there is a lot of activity in the nucleus. This activity doesn't take place all at once, but in stages or **phases**. There are four main phases of mitosis. It also does not happen without order, but in a specific **sequence**.

During the first phase, the chromosomes start to curl up and get thicker. In the next phase, the chromosomes begin to split. During the next phase, the split chromosomes become new chromosomes and move to opposite sides of the nucleus. During the final stage, the chromosomes uncurl. A new nuclear membrane forms around each new nucleus. When the final phase concludes, there are two new cells. How long do you **estimate** this takes?

Let's hope he's just going through a **phase**!

The Amoeba Family at Home

More New Life Science and Biology Words

fission

noun   making a new organism by splitting apart

function

noun   the purpose of something

mitosis

noun   the process in which a cell divides into two

phase

noun   one step or stage in a process

Other Useful Words

estimate

verb   to guess at the amount of something

noun   a guess at the amount of something

sequence

noun   a certain order of steps, events, numbers, or items

Apply the Strategy

Look at a chapter in your textbook that your teacher identifies. Use contrasts to help you figure out the meaning of any new words you find. Keep track of new words and contrasts in a chart.

Finish the Paragraph

Use the words in **bold** to finish the paragraph below. Write the correct words in the blanks. Discuss your choices with a partner.

diffusion   **functions**   **mitosis**   **phases**   **replication**   **transport**

For their science project Maria and Li built a large model of a cell. They wanted to show

the different parts of the cell as well as some of the cell's basic _____.

1

Using their model, they showed how the cell membrane allowed for _____,

2

or movement of substances in and out of the cell. They demonstrated the process of

_____ by putting a couple drops of food coloring into a bowl of

3

water and showing how it spread throughout the water until it was evenly colored.

Finally they explained how cells divide by going through the _____ of

4

_____. Another word for the making

5

of new cells is _____.

6

Word Challenge: Correct or Incorrect

Take turns with a partner reading the sentences below out loud. Write **C** if the sentence is correct, and write **I** if the sentence is incorrect. Rewrite the incorrect sentences. The first one has been done for you.

1   _I_   The gas spread through the room through the process of **transport**.

   The gas spread through the process of diffusion.

2   _____ **Fission** is the process bacteria use to reproduce.

_____

3   _____ Cells make copies of themselves through a process known as **fermentation**.

_____

4   _____ A **sequence** follows no specific order.

_____

Word Challenge: Finish the Idea

With a partner, take turns reading the incomplete sentences below. Write an ending for each. The first one has been done for you.

1   You can know that **fermentation** has happened when ___your muscles

   hurt after running really hard.

2   During **diffusion** _____

_____

3   We say that mitosis has a number of **phases** because _____

_____

4   You can **estimate** how long something will take by _____

_____

Categories

Write the words from the word bank in the correct boxes below. Some words may be used in more than one box. Discuss you answers with a partner.

| diffusion | fermentation | fission |
| mitosis | phase | replication | transport |

Cell Functions	Cell Reproduction

Word Study: The Suffix -al

When the suffix -al is added to a noun such as *observation*, it does two things:

- First, it makes the noun an adjective: *observational*.
- Second, it adds *of* or *like* to the word's meaning.

 You may need to change the spelling of a word before adding -al. Check a dictionary.

A. Add -al to each root noun to make a new word. Use a dictionary to check your spelling.

	+ -al
1 function	
2 phase	
3 sequence	

B. Fill each blank with the correct -al word from the chart.

1 This medicine will help his kidneys function. His kidneys will now be _____.

2 The events followed a certain sequence. They were _____.

3 The moon goes through phases. You could say the moon is _____.

24

The Language of Testing

How would you answer a question like this on a test?

Identify the process where gas or liquid passes through the cell membrane.

- A. mitosis
- B. metaphase
- C. osmosis
- D. diffusion

 Tip

The word *identify* means to point out or name. In a test question, it means that you need to choose or pick the correct answer.

Test Strategy: If you see a question that uses the word *identify*, rewrite it using the words *choose* or *pick*.

1 How could you say the question above in a different way?

_____

_____

Try the strategy again by asking these questions in a different way.

2 Identify the correct description for the term *fermentation*.

- A. energy production happens when no oxygen is present
- B. reproduction happens when no oxygen is present
- C. energy production happens when oxygen is present
- D. transport used by some organisms

3 Identify the term that means "the purpose or use for something."

- A. phase
- B. function
- C. fission
- D. reproduction

_____   _____

_____   _____

 In Your Vocabulary Journal

Find each of these words in your Life Science and Biology Vocabulary Journal. Working by yourself or with a partner, use the definitions from pages 21 and 22 of your Work Text to complete the rest of the entry for each word.

diffusion	estimate	fermentation	fission	function
mitosis	phase	replication	sequence	transport

Lesson 5 Heredity and Genetics

Read the passage below. Think about the meaning of the words printed in **bold**. Circle any words that end with *-ic* or *-ity*. Remember that *-ic* means *of* or "having to do with" and *-ity* refers to a way of being. Write what you think each words means next to it. The first one has been done for you.

A Genetic Family Tree

Vocabulary Strategy

Use familiar prefixes and suffixes to help you understand the meanings of new words.

has to do with

Many people take an interest in their family history. They find out information about people in their family who lived before them. The study of (**heredity**) is a lot like making a family tree. Heredity follows the **traits**, or characteristics that are passed through a family.

Genetic traits are characteristics that are passed through genes. Genes contain information that controls how a cell develops. Genes are in the cells of all organisms. They are the main way traits are passed from parent to child.

The study of genetics covers three main subjects. The first looks at how traits are passed from parents

to offspring. Using **probability**, or the likelihood of something happening, scientists can predict how likely it is that a trait will be passed on. Another kind of genetics looks at how DNA works. The last kind examines how organisms change over long periods of time.

New Life Science and Biology Words

genetic
adjective   having to do with the way features are passed from one organism to another

heredity
noun   the way in which features are passed from a parent to offspring

probability
noun   the chance or possibility that something will happen

trait
noun   a feature or characteristic of the way someone or something acts or looks

Now read this passage and look for prefixes or suffixes that can help you understand the words in **bold**. Circle any words that end in *-ed*, *-ation*, *-ive*. Write what you think each word means near it. Remember that *-ed* means that something has already happened, *-ation* refers to a process, and *-ive* means "belonging to."

 ## Gregor Mendel

Gregor Mendel was born in Austria in 1822. As a young man, Mendel became a priest. He tended the gardens at the monastery. Mendel became interested in how certain traits were **inherited**, or passed on from one **generation** of plant to the next, from parent to child. He experimented with pea plants and observed the traits in each generation. His work started the science of genetics.

Mendel **analyzed** or studied pairs of traits in generations of plants. He developed a theory that organisms carry traits from both parent organisms. Although he didn't name them, Mendel believed that something like genes caused traits to be passed on. He said that offspring carry two genes for each trait. The genes for the traits are either **dominant** or **recessive**. Dominant traits appear most often. But if two recessive or weak genes join together, the recessive trait will appear.

 ### More New Life Science and Biology Words

dominant

adjective   stronger or more noticeable

generation

noun   all the living things around the same age

inherit

verb   to receive something from a parent or grandparent

recessive

adjective   weaker and less noticeable

George's ears were a dominant **trait**.

 ### Other Useful Words

analyze

verb   to study information

calculate

verb   to add, subtract, multiply, or divide numbers

Apply the Strategy

Look at a chapter in your textbook that your teacher identifies. Use familiar suffixes to help you figure out the meaning of any new words you find.

27

Finish the Sentence

Use a word from the box to finish each sentence. Write the correct word on the line. Discuss your choices with a partner.

generation	**genetics**	**inherited**	**calculate**	**trait**

1 Her winning smile was her best characteristic or _____.

2 We added up all of the prices to _____ how much money we would have to pay.

3 My parents' _____ likes different music than mine.

4 I have red hair, just like my grandmother. I _____ it from her.

5 We studied _____, or how traits are passed on through genes.

analyzed	**probability**	**heredity**	**recessive**	**dominant**

6 They figured out that the chances or the _____ of that happening was about one in five.

7 Many people are right-handed. Being right handed is a _____ trait.

8 Because _____ traits are weaker, they often aren't passed on.

9 Tanya can trace her family's _____ back to 1792.

10 My grandmother studied or _____ old photos to see what traits had been passed on to us.

Word Challenge: Which Word?

With a partner, take turns saying the words listed below. Together, think of a statement for each one that gives a clue about its meaning. Write your statement next to the word. The first one has been done for you.

1 **dominant** _"I'm in charge!"_

2 **genetics** _____

3 **trait** _____

4 **recessive** _____

5 **calculate** _____

Word Challenge: What's Your Answer?

Take turns with a partner reading each question out loud and writing an answer on the line. Answer the questions in complete sentences. The first one has been done for you.

1 If your friend were part of your **generation**, what would that say about your friend?

It would mean we were born around the same time.

2 If you **inherited** a watch from your grandfather, what would that mean? _____

_____

3 If you had many of the same **traits** as your mother, what would that mean? _____

_____

4 If you had to figure out the **probability** of an event, what would you have to do? _____

_____

Synonyms and Antonyms

Write either a synonym or antonym for the vocabulary words below. Write only in the white boxes. Discuss your answers with a partner.

		Synonym	Antonym
1	inherit		
2	recessive		
3	probability		
4	calculate		
5	dominant		

Word Study: The Roots *her* and *gen*

When prefixes and suffixes are added to the roots *her* or *gen*, new words are formed: *generation, heredity*.

The root *gen* means starting or beginning.

The root *her* means to receive from those who came before.

A. Find words that have a *gen* or *her* root. Circle the root. Underline the prefixes and suffixes.

Rodney felt tired all the time. He went to the doctor to have some tests run. The doctor said that Rodney had a genetic blood disease. It was caused by heredity. Other people in his father's family had the same thing. Rodney had inherited the disease from his father.

Rodney hoped his children would not have the disease. He did not want the next generation of his family to feel as tired as he did.

B. Write sentences for a *gen* word and a *her* word. Write your own definition for each word you choose.

1 *gen* word: _____

Meaning: _____

2 *her* word: _____

Meaning: _____

The Language of Testing

How would you answer a question like this on a test?

What is (the purpose of) studying genetics?

    A. It helps us understand reproduction.
    B. It helps us understand cell function.
    C. It helps us understand how traits are passed between generations.
    D. It helps us understand what dominant and recessive traits are.

Tip

The word *purpose* can mean *reason* or *use*.

Test Strategy: If you see a question that uses the word *purpose*, rewrite it using the words *reason* or *use*.

1 How could you say the question above in a different way?

_____

_____

Try the strategy again by asking these questions in a different way.

2 What is the purpose of calculating probability?

    A. It allows us to make better predictions and hypotheses.
    B. It helps us graph statistics.
    C. It provides accurate data.
    D. It is a way of estimating an amount.

3 What is the main purpose of identifying traits?

    A. to help classify organisms
    B. to trace heredity
    C. to identify problems
    D. to provide data about certain people

_____   _____

_____   _____

_____   _____

In Your Vocabulary Journal

Find each of these words in your Life Science and Biology Vocabulary Journal. Working by yourself or with a partner, use the definitions from pages 26 and 27 of your Work Text to complete the rest of the entry for each word.

analyze	calculate	dominant	generation	genetic
heredity	inherit	probability	recessive	trait

Lesson 6 Diversity of Life

Read the passage below. Think about the meanings of the new words in **bold**. Underline any definitions that might help you figure out what the new words mean. The first one has been done for you.

Farm Colleges

Vocabulary Strategy

Look for definitions in the text to help you understand the meaning of new words.

Many universities have large farms where students **cultivate**, <u>or prepare fields and grow</u> crops. They set up large experiments in which they test things that affect crop growth such as water, type of soil, and sunlight. They look for any **variation**, or difference among the different crops. Sometimes these variations are caused by **mutation**, or when the genetic material in the plants changes.

Many crops are harmed by diseases and fungus. In addition, insects can harm the plants. Science labs at farm colleges try to figure out ways to prevent crops from being harmed. One way is to create a **hybrid**. A hybrid is a cross between two different varieties of the same plant. One type of corn, for example, might be able to fight off a certain fungus. Another variety of corn might not need much water. These two varieties are mixed together to create a hybrid corn that has the characteristics of both.

Thanks to the work at many colleges, farmers grow healthier crops, and we all eat better.

New Life Science and Biology Words

cultivate

verb to make the ground ready to grow crops or to grow crops

verb to develop something that could be good for you

hybrid

noun the offspring of two different species that has features of both

mutation

noun a sudden change in a plant or animal to a new kind of plant or animal

variation

noun a difference or change between two similar things

32

Now read this passage and practice the vocabulary strategy again. Underline any definitions in the passage that help you figure out what the new words in **bold** mean.

Dog Contests

All over the world, people hold contests to give prizes to special dogs. The people who hold these contests keep descriptions of every kind of dog. The dogs are judged **according to** or using the information in these descriptions. These descriptions tell traits such as color, personality, size, and shape for a certain kind of dog. There is great **diversity**, meaning many differences, among the different kinds of dogs. Just think of the differences between a tiny toy poodle and a giant Great Dane!

Each dog that enters one of these contests must have a **pedigree**, a list of its parents and their parents. Through careful breeding, each generation **acquires** the best characteristics of its breed. That means it receives the genes for specific traits. There are also negative traits that certain dogs may have. For example, some larger dog breeds have **disorders** with their hip joints. Disorders are problems or diseases. All of these **factors** affect how a dog does in the contest.

More New Life Science and Biology Words

acquire

   verb   to get or receive something new

disorder

   noun   an illness, fault, or problem

diversity

   noun   the amount of difference among things that are otherwise mostly alike

pedigree

   noun   a chart or list of all of the ancestors of an offspring

His **pedigree** gets the judges every time.

Other Useful Words

according (to)

   preposition as someone has said or written

factor

   noun   something that causes a result or outcome

Apply the Strategy

Look at a chapter in your textbook that your teacher identifies. Use definitions to help you figure out the meaning of any new words you find.

The Right Word

Read each sentence. Look at the word or phrase that is underlined. Write a word from the box that means the same or almost the same thing as the underlined part of the sentence. Discuss your answers with a partner.

mutation	disorder	diversity	hybrid

1. _____ One of the things that makes this country great is the <u>wide variety and number</u> of the people who live here.

2. _____ A mule is a <u>mixture</u> of a horse and a donkey.

3. _____ The <u>change</u> in the fruit flies was seen in the shape of their wings.

4. _____ The <u>illness or fault</u> affected the way that the cat was able to eat.

acquire	variation	pedigree	cultivate

5. _____ Many people who raise horses are concerned about <u>the horses' parents</u>.

6. _____ During their life cycle, amphibians <u>get</u> the ability to breathe with lungs.

7. _____ One of the great developments in civilization was when humans learned to <u>prepare the soil</u> and grow their own food.

8. _____ There is a large <u>difference</u> in the shape and color of needles on evergreen trees.

34

Word Challenge: True or False

Take turns with a partner reading the sentences below out loud. Write **T** next to each sentence that is true. Write **F** next to each sentence that is false.

1 __F__ An example of **diversity** is when everything is the same or similar.

An example of diversity would be when many things are different.

2 _____ The **hybrid** was the result of mixing two different kinds of soybeans.

_____

3 _____ Because the dog had no **pedigree**, we knew a lot about its parents.

_____

4 _____ The medicine was able to clear up the **disorder** that had made her skin red.

_____

Word Challenge: What's Your Answer?

Take turns with a partner reading each question out loud and writing an answer on the line. Answer the questions with complete sentences. The first one has been done for you.

1 What is something you would like to **acquire**? I would like to

acquire an MP-3 player.

2 How would you **cultivate** a garden? _____

_____

3 What might cause a **mutation**? _____

_____

4 What would be a **variation** between two T-shirts? _____

_____

Analogies

Use a word from the box to finish each sentence. Write the word on the line. Discuss your answers with a partner.

cultivate	acquire	disorder	mutation

1 Get is to _____ as give up is to lose.

2 Mow is to cutting grass as _____ is to digging soil.

3 Wellness is to healthy as sickness is to _____.

4 Change is to _____ as variety is to diversity.

Word Study: The Suffix -ation

When the suffix -ation is added to a root verb such as *mutate*, it does two things:

- First, it changes the verb to a noun: *mutation*.
- Second, it changes the word's meaning. The word now means the result of changing or mutating something.

> Drop the -e from the end of some words before adding -ation.
>
> Change the -y to -i at the end of other words before adding -ation.

A. Add the suffix -ation to each root verb to make a new word. Write a definition for each. Use a dictionary to check your spelling and definitions.

	+ -ation	Definition
1 cultivate		
2 mutate		
3 vary		

B. Write a new -ation word in each blank.

1 A _____ caused a few ears of corn to be dark blue.

2 My grandpa enjoys the growing, or _____, of tomatoes.

36

The Language of Testing

How would you answer a question like this on a test?

A bacteria is no longer controlled by a particular antibiotic. What does this **suggest**?

    A. The antibiotic was never really effective.
    B. The current bacteria is a mutation of the original bacteria.
    C. The antibiotic should not be used.
    D. The bacteria colony has grown.

 Tip

When *suggest* is used in a question it means that you should draw a conclusion about the information in the question.

Test Strategy: If you see a question that uses the word *suggest*, rewrite it to ask for your conclusion.

1 How could you say the question above in a different way?

_____

_____

Try the strategy again by asking these questions in a different way.

2 What does it suggest about a civilization if the people have learned to cultivate the soil and grow crops?

    A. The people are nomadic.
    B. The people will probably settle in one place.
    C. The people are hunter-gatherers.
    D. The culture is very advanced.

_____

_____

_____

3 An ecological community is very diverse. What does this suggest?

    A. There are many species.
    B. The climate is very warm.
    C. The community is located in the rain forests of Brazil.
    D. Too many animals live in the area.

_____

_____

_____

In Your Vocabulary Journal

Find each of these words in your Life Science and Biology Vocabulary Journal. Working by yourself or with a partner, use the definitions from pages 32 and 33 of your Work Text to complete the rest of the entry for each word.

according (to)	acquire	cultivate	disorder	diversity
factor	hybrid	mutation	pedigree	variation

Lesson 7 Change Over Time

Read the passage below. Think about the meanings of the new words in **bold**. Underline any examples or descriptions you find that might help you figure out the meaning of the new words. The first one has been done for you.

Vocabulary Strategy

Use examples and descriptions to help you figure out the meanings of new words. Look for clues like *for example*, *like*, or *such as*.

Charles Darwin

Charles Darwin was a scientist who lived in the 1800s. He developed the theory of **evolution**. This theory stated that the plants and animals on Earth today developed from simpler forms of life. For example, the theory states that one-celled organisms developed into many-celled organisms. These then developed into more complicated plants and animals over millions of years. Darwin also wrote that all species have a common **origin**.

In his famous book *The Origin of Species,* Darwin wrote about **adaptation**. Plants and animals change or adapt to a new environment. The saying "the survival of the fittest" is based on Darwin's ideas about natural **selection**. Darwin wrote that weaker animal and plant species die out and are replaced by stronger species.

Darwin's ideas caused arguments when they were discussed in the 19th century. Many of his ideas are still argued about today.

New Life Science and Biology Words

adaptation

noun the process of changing, or a change that has been made

evolution

noun the process by which plants and animals develop and change over millions of years

origin

noun the beginning or source of something

selection

noun the act of choosing something

Now read this passage and practice the vocabulary strategy again. Underline the examples and descriptions in the passage. Draw an arrow from each to the new word it describes.

Paleontology

Paleontology (pay lee ahn **tah** luh jee) is a branch of science that studies plants and animals that lived thousands, even millions of years ago. The scientists who work in this field study **fossils**, remains of animals and plants that have died and been preserved in stone. You can see fossils of leaves, insects, small animals, and even large bones. Paleontologists study and **interpret** the information fossils provide to learn about life during different periods of time.

Most of the plants and animals that have become fossils are **extinct**. Dinosaurs are an example of extinct animals. No one knows for sure why they died out, but it was probably because of some sort of major change in the weather or temperature. Other animals, such as mammals, lived because they had the **advantage** of being able to adapt or change more easily.

Paleontologists have learned that as one species of plant or animal died out, another took its place. This kept an **equilibrium**, or balance in the food web millions of years ago.

More New Life Science and Biology Words

advantage
  noun   a helpful trait or characteristic that others may not have

equilibrium
  noun   a balance between two or more forces or things

extinct
  adjective   having to do with a species that is no longer alive

fossil
  noun   remains of a dead plant or animal that have been preserved in stone

"That's not a **fossil**, that's a two week old sandwich!"

Other Useful Words

confirm
  verb   to prove that something is true

interpret
  verb   to decide the meaning of something and explain it

Apply the Strategy

Look at a chapter in your textbook that your teacher identifies. Use explanations and descriptions in the text to help you figure out the meaning of any new words you find. You may want to draw pictures to help you remember what the new words mean.

Finish the Sentence

Use a word from the box to finish each sentence. Write the correct word on the line. Discuss your choices with a partner.

advantage	evolution	extinct	fossil

1 We found a _____ of a leaf in a stone down by the river.

2 Some scientists believe life on Earth developed through _____.

3 Our team had the _____ because their team had two hurt players.

4 An ivory-billed woodpecker, which was believed to have been dead,

or _____, was seen in Arkansas.

equilibrium	selection	origin	adaptation

5 The shark's _____ goes back millions of years.

6 When we got off the spinning ride we were dizzy, and it took a while to get

our _____.

7 It took Lupe several minutes to make her final _____ of all of the flavors

of ice cream.

8 Many organisms were able to survive through _____ and change.

40

Word Challenge: Which Word?

With a partner, take turns saying the words listed below. Together, think of a statement for each one that gives a clue about its meaning. Write your statement next to the word. The first one has been done for you.

1 adaptation *"I'm all about change."* _____

2 fossil _____

3 equilibrium _____

4 origin _____

5 interpretation _____

Word Challenge: Correct or Incorrect

Take turns with a partner reading the sentences below out loud. Write **C** if the sentence is correct, and write **I** if the sentence is incorrect. Rewrite the incorrect sentences. The first one has been done for you.

1 __*I*__ Some animals died off because they had an **advantage**.

Some animals lived because they had an advantage.

2 _____ A theory can be **confirmed**.

_____

3 _____ I'm glad that dinosaurs are not **extinct**.

_____

4 _____ When you decide on something, you make a **selection**.

_____

Categories

Write the words from the word bank in the correct boxes below. Some words may be used in more than one box.

adaptation	advantage	equilibrium
evolution	extinct	fossil	selection

Changing	Not Alive

Word Study: The Suffix -ate

When the suffix -ate is added to a noun such as equilibrium, it does two things:

- First, it makes the noun a verb: equilibrate.
- Second, it adds the meaning "to become" or "to come into."

equilibrium (n.) a balance between two or more forces or things

equilibrate (v.) to come into a state of equilibrium

A. Add the suffix -ate to each word and write a definition for each. Use the dictionary to check your spelling and your definitions.

	+ -ate	Definition
1 stimulus		
2 origin		
3 replica		

B. Write an -ate word in each blank. Use the words from the chart.

1 Bobbie wanted to trace her family's roots. The first question asked was, "Where did my family

_____?"

2 Joe was sleepy. He needed something to _____ him.

3 Cells split to _____, or make copies of themselves.

The Language of Testing

How would you answer a question like this on a test?

What is something that **compares closely to** evolution?

- A. balanced systems
- B. natural selection
- C. paleontology
- D. biology

 Tip

The phrase *compares closely to* means "is most like."

Test Strategy: If you see a question with the phrase *compares closely to*, rewrite it using the phrase *is most like*.

1 How could you say the question above in a different way?

_____

_____

Try the strategy again by asking these questions in a different way.

2 What term compares closely to *equilibrium*?

- A. unbalanced
- B. balanced
- C. equal
- D. evolution

3 Which term compares most closely to *extinct*?

- A. endangered
- B. successful
- C. nonexistent
- D. living

_____

_____

_____

_____

_____

_____

 In Your Vocabulary Journal

Find each of these words in your Life Science and Biology Vocabulary Journal. Working by yourself or with a partner, use the definitions from pages 38 and 39 of your Work Text to complete the rest of the entry for each word.

adaptation	advantage	confirm	equilibrium	evolution
extinct	fossil	interpret	origin	selection

Interactions in Nature

Read the passage below. Think about the meaning of the words printed in **bold**. Circle any words that start with *eco-*, *bio-*, *sym-*, or *inter-*. Remember that *eco-* refers to the environment and *inter-* means *between* or *among*. Write what you think each of the circled words means next to it. The first one has been done for you.

Of Ants and Acacias

Vocabulary Strategy

Use familiar prefixes and suffixes to help you understand the meanings of new words.

action between →

Of all the (interactions) between species, one of the most fascinating is **symbiosis**. While many species are in **competition** for food or shelter, those in a symbiotic relationship benefit each other and themselves at the same time.

Symbiosis can be found in practically any **ecosystem**. Some examples include cleaner fish and the fish they clean, bacteria in the intestines of mammals that break down food, and insects that help pollinate flowers.

A clear example of plant and insect symbiosis is the relationship between a type of acacia tree that grows in Mexico and Central America, and a species of ant. The tree lacks the ability some acacias have to help guard against predators and competition from other plants. However, it does have something special — ants! The stinging ants fiercely defend the tree by attacking any herbivores or insects that try to eat it. The ants also cut back vines that would choke or crowd the tree.

In return, the acacia provides the ants with a place to live. It also produces two special foods just for the ants. It's a clear case of symbiosis!

New Life Science and Biology Words

competition

noun   the act of trying to succeed over someone or something

ecosystem

noun   the relationship between organisms and their environment

interaction

noun   the way in which two or more things affect one another

symbiosis

noun   a relationship between two organisms in which at least one is dependent on the other

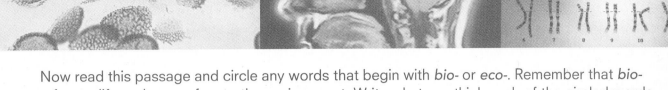

Now read this passage and circle any words that begin with *bio-* or *eco-*. Remember that *bio-* refers to life and *eco-* refers to the environment. Write what you think each of the circled words means next to it.

 ## Extreme Habitats

You wouldn't believe the places that some organisms call home! Over the past decades, scientists have discovered life in places that were once believed to be too hot, too cold, or too salty for life to exist.

Who would have thought, for example, that anything could live in the hot springs of Yellowstone National Park? It turns out there are a number of bacteria that thrive in very hot, or even boiling water, some of it full of sulfuric acid. In each **habitat**, organisms find their own particular **niche**. Different bacteria live in different parts of the springs. Some live in cooler areas, while others live in warmer areas. Each

takes advantage of its different position in the **ecology** of the hot spring.

Scientists used to think that the **biosphere** went just a few meters below the earth's surface. They thought life would be impossible deeper underground. Recently, however, bacteria have been found growing in cracks in the rock crevices kilometers below the earth's surface.

It really seems like there is almost no place on our planet too extreme for life!

Hot! Hot! Hot!

Deep in the earth!

EXTREME Habitats! Which **niche** is for you?

 ## More New Life Science and Biology Words

biosphere

noun   Earth's land and air where life can exist

ecology

noun   the study of living things and their environment

habitat

noun   the place where a plant or animal usually lives and grows

niche

noun   a certain place or position occupied by an organism

Other Useful Words

assemble

verb   to put parts together

evaluate

verb   to determine something's value or importance

Apply the Strategy

Look at a chapter in your textbook that your teacher identifies. Use familiar prefixes and suffixes to help you figure out the meaning of any new words you find.

Matching

Write the letter of the word or phrase that best completes the sentence. Discuss your choices with a partner.

Group A

1. Coral reefs provide a _____ for many colorful fish and invertebrates.

2. The _____ between parasite and host only benefits the parasite.

3. Scientists have found that the _____ of wetlands is rich and diverse.

4. The relationship between a bee and a flower is an example of _____.

5. We had to read the directions many times before we could _____ the bike.

Group B

A. habitat

B. symbiosis

C. ecology

D. assemble

E. interaction

Group A

6. When two species share an ecological _____, they must compete for resources.

7. Native plants often face _____ from exotic species.

8. Cloud forests are a unique _____ found in some tropical mountain areas.

9. The _____ supports life even in harsh environments such as the desert.

10. The judges agreed on how they would _____ the contestants.

Group B

F. competition

G. niche

H. ecosystem

I. evaluate

J. biosphere

Word Challenge: Finish the Idea

With a partner, take turns reading the incomplete sentences below. Write an ending for each. The first one has been done for you.

1 People who study **ecology** are probably interested in ___how animals and plants___

___live together.___

2 There is fierce **competition** for resources when _____

_____

3 The earth's **biosphere** includes _____

_____

4 Animals lose their **habitat** when _____

_____

Word Challenge: What's Your Answer?

Take turns with a partner reading each question out loud and writing the answer on the line. Answer the questions in complete sentences. The first one has been done for you.

1 What do you think happens when two organisms share the same **niche**?
___They fight over resources.___

2 How is **symbiosis** different from a predator and prey relationship? _____

_____

3 What do you think it means if an **ecosystem** is fragile? _____

_____

4 How would you **assemble** a group of people for a project? _____

_____

47

Extend the Meaning

Write the letter of the word or phrase that best completes each sentence. Discuss your choices with a partner.

1 **Competition** between species means they _____.
   a. live together in a delicate balance
   b. eat each other
   c. try to win in a battle for survival

2 An animals' **habitat** is _____.
   a. where it lives
   b. what it eats
   c. how it gets food

3 **Symbiosis** between two species benefits _____.
   a. neither partner
   b. both partners
   c. one partner

4 The **interaction** between two living things is _____.
   a. how they help each other
   b. how they compete for resources
   c. how they affect each other

Word Study: The Prefix *bio-*

When the prefix *bio-* is added to a noun such as *sphere*, it changes the noun's meaning. The word now names something that has to do with life.

 **sphere** (n.) a globe, or an area in which something exists
biosphere (n.) an area in which life exists

A. Circle the *bio-* words in the story.

I'm reading a biography about an astronaut whose rocket exploded while he was exploring the upper part of the biosphere. The doctors used bioelectronics, or bionics, to allow him to use his damaged legs and one of his arms again. The doctors keep track of the astronaut's health with a biofeedback machine attached to his watch.

B. Fill each blank with a *bio-* word from the story.

1 The book about the astronaut's life is his _____.

2 You can keep track of life systems with a _____ machine.

3 Electronics that can be used to heal bodies are called _____.

48

The Language of Testing

How would you answer a question like this on a test?

What is the **major cause** of increased competition between two species?

    A. loss of habitat
    B. climate change
    C. increased aggression
    D. shortage of food

 Tip

The word *cause* means the reason something happened. The *major cause* is the most important reason why something happened.

Test Strategy: If any questions contain the phrase *the major cause of something*, restate the question to ask for the main reason for something. You can also add the phrase *is a major cause of* to each answer choice to test if it is right or wrong.

1 What phrase would you use to test each answer choice above?

_____

_____

Try the strategy again by adding a text phrase to the answer choices below. Write your test phrase below each question.

2 What is one major cause of global warming?

    A. space exploration
    B. the burning of fossil fuels
    C. increased heat of the sun
    D. tree planting

3 What is a major cause of soil erosion?

    A. nuclear energy
    B. symbiosis
    C. deforestation
    D. cold weather

_____   _____

_____   _____

_____   _____

In Your Vocabulary Journal

Find each of these words in your Life Science and Biology Vocabulary Journal. Working by yourself or with a partner, use the definitions from pages 44 and 45 of your Work Text to complete the rest of the entry for each word.

assemble	biosphere	competition	ecology	ecosystem
evaluate	habitat	interaction	niche	symbiosis

Simple Organisms and Fungi

Read the passage below. Think about the meanings of the new words printed in **bold**. Underline any examples or descriptions you find that might help you figure out the meaning of the new words. The first one has been done for you.

What We Can't See Won't Hurt Us . . . or Will It?

Vocabulary Strategy

Use examples and descriptions to help you figure out the meanings of new words. Look for clues like *for example*, *like*, or *such as.* Look for pictures that might show what a new word means, too.

All around us are microbes. These are simple organisms too small to be seen with the human eye. Some help us, some have no effect on us, and some can do a lot of damage.

Perhaps the best-known of these microbes are **bacteria**. Some bacteria can cause diseases, such as <u>strep throat, pneumonia, and tuberculosis</u>.

Parasites can also be trouble. Lice and tapeworms are all examples of parasites that make humans sick. People are not the only **hosts**, however. In fact, all living things are attacked by parasites. Dogs, for example, are hosts for heartworms, which are parasites.

Perhaps the strangest microbes are **viruses**. On their own, viruses are barely even alive. They cannot eat, move, or reproduce. Once inside a host, however, they use the host's own cells to reproduce and thrive. Viruses cause many serious diseases, including the common cold and chicken pox.

But try not to worry! Medical researchers are always working hard to find ways to protect us from these unseen attackers.

New Life Science and Biology Words

bacteria

noun   one-celled organisms that live in air, soil, water, animals, and plants

host

noun   an organism that is home to another form of life, or someone who serves or entertains guests

verb   to serve or entertain guests, or to be a home for another organism

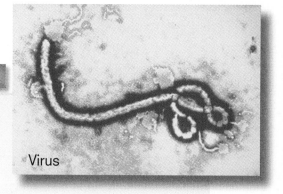
Virus

parasite

noun   an organism that lives on or in another organism and feeds on it

virus

noun   a tiny organism that causes disease in plants and animals

Now read this passage and practice the vocabulary strategy again. Underline examples and descriptions in the passage. Draw an arrow from each to the word it describes.

What Is a Mushroom?

A mushroom is not a fruit or a vegetable. It's a **fungus**. Other examples of *fungi*, the plural of *fungus*, include mold and yeast.

Fungi have characteristics of both plants and animals. Like plants, they have a type of root. Unlike plants, however, they cannot produce their own energy. All plants, and even **algae** and seaweed are able to create their own food.

Because they can't make energy, fungi have to eat, just like animals do. However, they live directly on their food source. They dissolve the food source and absorb its nutrients. The food source could be rotting wood or even bits of dead skin between your toes. Yes, athlete's foot is a fungus.

Mold is a fungus that grows on food and makes it spoil. It does have some useful purposes as well, though. The medicine penicillin is made from a mold. Molds, like other fungi, reproduce through cells called **spores**. Spores are a bit like seeds, but are just one cell.

Dad! That **mold** and **fungus** is my science project!

More New Life Science and Biology Words

algae
   noun   very simple plants that grow in water and have no leaves or roots

fungus
   noun   an organism that is like a plant but does not have leaves, seeds, or flowers

mold
   noun   an organism that grows on rotting food or other warm, slightly wet objects

spore
   noun   a cell that some plants and fungi use to reproduce

Other Useful Words

focus
   verb   to examine closely or to concentrate on
   noun   the center of activity or attention

summarize
   verb   to state the main points in a shortened way

Apply the Strategy

Look at a chapter in your textbook that your teacher identifies. Use explanations, descriptions, and pictures in the text to help you figure out the meaning of any new words you find.

Finish the Paragraph

Use the words in **bold** to finish the paragraph below. Write the correct words in the blanks. Discuss your choices with a partner.

algae   **bacteria**   **fungus**   **host**   **mold**   **parasites**   **focus**

You wouldn't think that microbes and other simple organisms would be good to eat, but

sometimes they are. A mushroom, for example, is a _____, and you
(1)

know how often they show up in omelets and on burgers! The single-celled organisms

that turn milk into yogurt are _____. A particular kind of
(2)

_____ that grows on blue cheese gives it its special flavor. The Japanese
(3)

often use seaweed in their cooking. Seaweed is a type of _____.
(4)

Sometimes the tables get turned, however, and WE are the ones

being eaten. A human can be a _____
(5)

for _____ such as a tapeworm. Not all
(6)

parasites _____ on animals, however.
(7)

Some are even vegetarian. These attack food crops.

Word Challenge: True or False

Take turns with a partner reading the sentences below out loud. Write **T** next to each sentence that is true. Write **F** next to each sentence that is false. Rewrite the false sentences. The first one has been done for you.

1. __F__ A **parasite** is an organism that is attacked by another organism.

   A parasite lives in or on another organism.

2. _____ **Mold** is a type of fungus that can grow on moist objects, such as cheese or bread.

   _____

3. _____ **Algae** are water plants with leaves and roots.

   _____

4. _____ When you **focus** on something, you don't pay very much attention to it.

   _____

Word Challenge: What's Your Answer?

Take turns with a partner reading each question out loud and writing the answer on the line. Answer the questions in complete sentences. The first one has been done for you.

1. What kinds of organisms use **spores** to reproduce? _Mushrooms and_

   mold use spores to reproduce.

2. How is a natural **host** like someone who hosts a party? _____

   _____

3. What kinds of places do **bacteria** live in? _____

   _____

4. Why is it good to **summarize** things you read? _____

   _____

Word Connections

In the spaces at the top of the wheel, write the words from the box that connect to the center word or idea. In the shaded spaces at the bottom of the wheel, write the words that do not connect. Discuss your answers with a partner.

focus	virus	spore	parasite	algae	bacteria

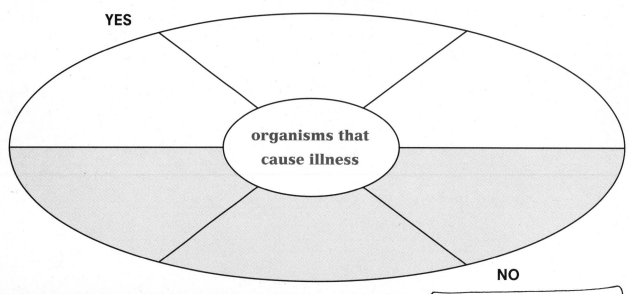

YES

organisms that cause illness

NO

Word Study: The Prefixes *mega-* and *micro-*

When a prefix *mega-* or *micro-* is added to a noun, it changes the noun's meaning.
- *Mega-* adds the meaning *big*.
- *Micro-* adds the meaning *small*.

When the root noun begins with a vowel, you may need to add a hyphen between the prefix and the root.

algae (n.) very simple plants that grow in water and have no leaves or roots
mega-algae (n.) a large algae
micro-algae (n.) a small algae

A. Add the *mega-* and *micro-* prefixes to make new words.

		+ *mega-*	+ *micro-*
1	bacteria		
2	fungus		
3	spore		

B. Fill each blank with a *mega-* or *micro-* word from the chart.

1 A really big mushroom would be a _____.

2 Most spores are very tiny. They can be called _____.

54

The Language of Testing

How would you answer a question like this on a test?

Which of the following are **not** simple organisms?

   A. seaweeds
   B. molds
   C. bacteria
   D. insects

 Tip

The phrase *which of the following* means that you need to choose one of the answers listed (A, B, C, or D) to answer the question. The word *not* means you need to choose the one answer choice that is not true.

Test Strategy: If a question contains the phrase *which of the following*, you can rewrite it to start with *who, what* or *where.*

1 How could you say the question above in a different way?

_____

_____

Try the strategy again by asking these questions in a different way.

2 Which of the following scientists do not study living things?

   A. entomologists
   B. biologists
   C. geologists
   D. mycologists

3 Which of the following are not plants?

   A. moss
   B. grass
   C. ivy
   D. mushrooms

_____

_____

_____

_____

_____

_____

 ## In Your Vocabulary Journal

Find each of these words in your Life Science and Biology Vocabulary Journal. Working by yourself or with a partner, use the definitions from pages 50 and 51 of your Work Text to complete the rest of the entry for each word.

algae	bacteria	focus	fungus	host
mold	parasite	spore	summarize	virus

Read the passage below. Think about the meanings of the new words in **bold**. Underline any familiar root words within the new words that might help you figure out what they mean. Write what the root means near the word. The first one has been done for you.

Seaweed

Vocabulary Strategy

Use familiar root words to help you unlock the meaning of unfamiliar words in the same family. For example, *gene* can help you unlock the meaning of *genetic*, *generate*, and *generation*.

Although they are similar to plants, seaweeds are actually **algae**. Unlike plants, they do not have roots, stems, leaves, or flowers. They also have no **vascular** system. All parts of the seaweed touch the water, so they can take up everything they need directly. They do not need the veins or tubes that plants use to transport water and food.

Like plants, seaweeds have the sunlight-catching material **chlorophyll**. They use this to carry out **photosynthesis**. The chlorophyll has a green color, but some seaweed contains other **pigments** that absorb light. These red, brown, blue, and gold

light

materials give seaweed its variety of beautiful colors.

Seaweeds have some wonderful names, too. Sea Whistle, Bladderwrack, Dabberlocks, Sea Lettuce, Harpoon Weed, Irish Moss, Nori, and Spongeweed are a few examples. As the names **indicate**, or suggest, seaweed are very diverse. Some are tiny and float free, while others reach lengths of 30 meters!

New Life Science and Biology Words

photosynthesis
  noun   the process by which a plant makes food by using sunlight and air

pigment
  noun   a material that gives something its color

pollination
  noun   the process of moving pollen from the male part of a plant to a female part of a plant

vascular
  adjective   having to do with the system of veins and tubes in animals and plants that carry blood and other fluids

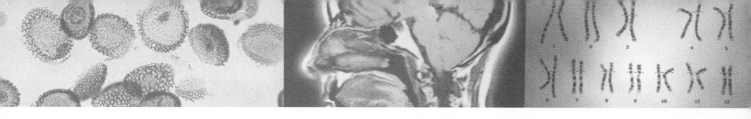

Now read this passage and practice the vocabulary strategy again. Circle familiar root words that are found in larger, unfamiliar words. Write the meaning of the circled root word near it.

Hybrids

A **hybrid** is something with mixed parents or mixed parts. A hybrid car, for example, runs on both gas and electric power. In **botany**, the study of plants, hybrids are plants with parents from different plant varieties. Botanists create hybrids in order to solve problems. For example, after **consulting** with farmers, they might find out that a certain kind of tomato tastes good, but does not last long. They might then mix that kind of tomato with one that does not spoil easily.

To create a hybrid, botanists and farmers can't rely on the natural means of **pollination**.

Instead of letting bees or a breeze take the pollen from the male to the female part of the plant, they take control of the process. They take the pollen from one plant and **fertilize** the other plant by hand.

Quite often, the resulting hybrid's seeds do not **germinate**. This is because the two parent plants are so genetically different. Since the hybrid's seeds won't open up and grow, the process of creating the hybrid has to be repeated every year.

More New Life Science and Biology Words

botany

   noun   the study of plants

chlorophyll

   noun   the material in a plant that makes it green

fertilize

   verb   to make soil richer so that plants will grow better, or to bring together an egg with the male reproductive cell to produce offspring

germinate

   verb   to begin to grow from a seed

Other Useful Words

consult

   verb   to ask or check for information or advice

indicate

   verb   to point out or point to something

"I think it might be time for Mr. Alonzo to stop **fertilizing** his flowers."

Apply the Strategy

Look at a chapter in your textbook that your teacher identifies. Use familiar root words to help you figure out the meaning of any new words you find.

The Right Word

Read each sentence. Look at the word or phrase that is underlined. Write one of the words from the box that means the same or almost the same thing as the underlined part of the sentence. Discuss your answers with a partner.

botany	indicates	chlorophyll	germinate	pollination

1 _____ The radish seeds were the first to <u>open up and start growing</u>.

2 _____ Leaves are green because of the <u>liquid that helps them change light into energy</u> they contain.

3 _____ Cucumber farmers keep bee hives near their fields so the bees can help with <u>the movement of pollen from one plant to another</u>.

4 _____ The red light on the stove <u>points out</u> when it is hot enough to cook something.

5 _____ I chose a class in <u>the study of plants</u> to fill my science requirement.

consulted	fertilizer	photosynthesis	pigment	vascular

6 _____ Because of the green <u>color</u> in chlorophyll, almost all leaves are green.

7 _____ A plant uses its <u>tube or vein-like</u> system to carry water and food.

8 _____ If I add <u>something to enrich the soil</u> to my lawn, the grass will grow better.

9 _____ We <u>asked for advice from</u> Benjamin's father about our problems with the coach.

10 _____ Unlike plants, fungi cannot perform <u>the process of making food from air and water</u>.

Word Challenge: Finish the Idea

With a partner, take turns reading the incomplete sentences below. Write an ending for each sentence that shows that you understand the meaning of the new words. The first one has been done for you.

1 People **fertilize** their gardens to _make them grow better._

2 To perform **photosynthesis**, plants need _____

_____

3 **Pollination** is necessary because _____

_____

4 For advice about my future, I would **consult** with _____

_____

Word Challenge: Correct or Incorrect

Take turns with a partner reading the sentences below out loud. Write **C** if the sentence is correct, and write **I** if the sentence is incorrect. Rewrite the incorrect sentences. The first one has been done for you.

1 _C_ A seed will only **germinate** given the right conditions.

2 _____ Taking classes in **botany** is a good way to learn about insects.

_____

3 _____ She wore a hat to **indicate** her bad hair cut.

_____

4 _____ Something containing a red **pigment** will look red.

_____

Categories

Write the words from the word bank in the correct boxes below. Some words may be used in more than one box. Discuss your choices with a partner.

| chlorophyll | fertilize | germinate | photosynthesis |
| pigment | pollination | vascular | |

Plant Structure, Appearance, and Energy Production	Plant Reproduction

Word Study: The Suffix *-ize*

When the suffix *-ize* is added to a root word such as *photosynthesis*, it does two things:

- First, it makes the noun a verb: *photosynthesize*.
- Second, it adds the meaning *become* or *make* to the word.

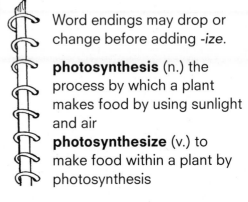

Word endings may drop or change before adding *-ize*.

photosynthesis (n.) the process by which a plant makes food by using sunlight and air
photosynthesize (v.) to make food within a plant by photosynthesis

Add the suffix *-ize* to each word and create your own definition for the new word. Use the dictionary to check your spelling and definitions.

	+ *-ize*	Definition
1 fertile		
2 hybrid		
3 theory		
4 hypothesis		

The Language of Testing

How would you answer a question like this on a test?

The terms *pollination, stamen,* and *anther* are

(associated with)

    A. nonvascular plants
    B. molds and mildews
    C. plant reproduction
    D. evolution

 Tip

When the phrase *associated with* is used in a question, it means *related to* or *connected to*.

Test Strategy: If a question contains the phrase *associated with*, rewrite it using the phrases *related to* or *connected to*.

1 How could you say the question above in a different way?

_____

_____

Try the strategy again by asking these questions in a different way.

2 Chlorophyll, sunlight, and carbon dioxide are associated with

    A. bacteria
    B. waste byproducts
    C. photosynthesis
    D. pigmentation

3 Botanists are associated with

    A. economics
    B. flower arranging
    C. science
    D. real estate

_____

_____

_____

_____

In Your Vocabulary Journal

Find each of these words in your Life Science and Biology Vocabulary Journal. Working by yourself or with a partner, use the definitions from pages 56 and 57 of your Work Text to complete the rest of the entry for each word.

| botany | chlorophyll | consult | fertilize | germinate |
| indicate | photosynthesis | pigment | pollination | vascular |

Lesson 11 The Food Web

Read the passage below. Think about the meanings of the words printed in **bold**. Create associations between familiar words and the new words to help you remember what the new words mean. Write these associations near the new words. The first one has been done for you.

What Did Dinosaurs Have for Dinner?

Vocabulary Strategy

Create associations between things you know and the new words to "anchor" your understanding of the new word. You can complete a Word Anchor chart for some of the new words.

Scientists who study dinosaur bones can tell what certain kinds of dinosaurs ate. They do this by looking at fossilized dinosaur teeth and noticing if they were mostly for chewing, crushing, or tearing.

Their research indicates that most dinosaurs were **herbivores**. *cows* In other words, they ate plants. The dinosaur herbivores had teeth suited for stripping leaves off branches, grinding leaves and roots, or uprooting plants.

A smaller number of dinosaurs were **carnivores**. Carnivores eat meat. Most carnivores are **scavengers** rather than hunters.

This means that they eat something that they have not killed themselves. A carnivore that comes across a dead animal will not turn down a free meal!

Evidence also shows that there were a few dinosaurs that were **omnivores**. Omnivores eat both plants and animals. As scientists keep finding fossils, our understanding of dinosaurs will keep on growing.

New Life Science and Biology Words

carnivore
noun an organism that eats mostly meat

herbivore
noun an organism that eats mostly plants

omnivore
noun an organism that eats both plants and meat

scavenger
noun an organism that feeds on dead animals that it has not killed

Now read this passage and practice the vocabulary strategy again. Write near the new words any associations you can create or find to anchor the meaning of the new words.

The Circle of Life

Every living organism, plant or animal, needs **nutrients**. Nutrients are things that provide necessary energy for life and growth. Nutrients for a plant come from the air, water, and soil.

Plants are known as **producers** because they make their own food and serve as food for other organisms. **Consumers** eat plants and other organisms, using up resources rather than making them. There are different types of consumers. The largest group eats only plants. Next up on the food chain are those that eat the plant-eaters. At the top of the chain are the animals that eat other animals that eat meat.

All living things eventually die. What happens to an organism that dies? This is where the **decomposers** come in. Decomposers are organisms that help **prepare** material so that it can go back into the soil as nutrients. Decomposers like bacteria and fungi break down organic matter from a dead organism. Soon, nothing is left but its building blocks. These go back into the soil and the circle continues.

More New Life Science and Biology Words

consumer

noun an organism that eats or uses up something

decomposer

noun an organism that helps break down dead matter

nutrient

noun a substance that a plant or animal needs to help it live and grow

producer

noun an organism that manufactures its own food and serves as food to other organisms

"Do you have anything for **herbivores**?"

Other Useful Words

emphasize

verb to show that something is important

prepare

verb to get ready for something ahead of time

Apply the Strategy

Look at a chapter in your textbook that your teacher identifies. Use associations and word anchors to help you build your understanding of any new words you find.

Matching

Finish the sentences in Group A with words from Group B. Write the letter of the word on the line. Discuss your choices with a partner.

Group A

1. Dark green, leafy vegetables are full of _____.

2. Plants and algae are _____ because they are food to other organisms.

3. Our teacher uses colored pens to _____ important information.

4. _____ use resources and eat other organisms or organic matter.

5. _____ eat both plants and animals.

Group B

A. producers

B. Consumers

C. Omnivores

D. chlorophyll

E. emphasize

Group A

6. Lions, tigers, and other big cats are _____.

7. _____ eat animals that have died on their own or been killed by others.

8. We cleaned the house yesterday to _____ for the guests who are coming today.

9. Dead leaves are broken down by the _____ on the forest floor.

10. _____ like cows have to eat a large amount of plant material every day to stay healthy.

Group B

F. prepare

G. carnivores

H. Herbivores

I. decomposers

J. Scavengers

Word Challenge: True or False

Take turns with a partner reading the sentences below out loud. Write **T** next to each sentence that is true. Write **F** next to each sentence that is false. Rewrite the false sentences. The first one has been done for you.

1 __T__ An **omnivore** might eat a cheeseburger and a salad.

2 _____ A **scavenger** kills its prey and then leaves it.

_____

3 _____Only carnivores need **nutrients** in order to grow.

_____

4 _____ Some people speak more loudly when they want to **emphasize** what they are saying.

_____

5 _____ Plants are not **consumers** because they make their own food.

_____

Word Challenge: Which Word?

With a partner, take turns saying the words listed below. Together, think of a statement for each one that gives a clue about its meaning. Write your statement next to the word. The first one has been done for you.

1 herbivore _"I like to eat leaves."_____

2 scavenger _____

3 decomposer _____

4 producer _____

5 nutrient _____

Synonyms and Antonyms

Write either a synonym or antonym for the vocabulary words below. In some cases you may be able to provide both. Discuss your answers with a partner.

		Synonym	Antonym
1	consumer		
2	nutrient		
3	prepare		
4	scavenger		
5	emphasize		

Word Study: The Suffix -vore

The suffix -vore means *eater*.
When the suffix -vore is added to root words, new words are formed: *carnivore, omnivore.*

The root *omni* means *all* or *everything.*

The root *herbi* means *plants.*

The root *carni* means *meat.*

A. Find words that have the suffix -*vore*. Circle the suffix. Underline the root.

Gemma's class was learning about food webs. They learned that plants are producers. Animals that eat the plants are herbivores. Omnivores are animals that eat both animals and plants. Carnivores are animals that eat other animals. Every life form has its place in a food web.

B. Choose two -*vore* words from the paragraph to use in sentences.

1 -*vore* word: _____

Sentence: _____

2 -*vore* word: _____

Sentence: _____

The Language of Testing

How would you answer a question like this on a test?

What role do decomposers play in the food chain?
Choose the 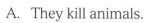best answer.

A. They kill animals.
B. They break down decaying organic matter.
C. They feed plants and animals.
D. They eat both plants and animals.

 Tip

When the word *best* is used in a question, you should look for the answer that is the most correct. More than one answer might be slightly correct, but only one answer is the most correct, or the *best*.

Test Strategy: If a question asks you to choose the *best* answer, restate the question using the phrase *most correct*.

1 How could you say the question above in a different way?

_____

_____

Try the strategy again by asking these questions in a different way.

2 In which groups do humans belong? Choose the best answer.

A. vegetarians
B. carnivores
C. omnivores
D. scavengers

3 Even producers need nutrients. What do they consume? Choose the best answer.

A. water and air
B. sunlight
C. minerals from the soil or water
D. sunlight, air, water, and minerals

_____

_____

_____

In Your Vocabulary Journal

Find each of these words in your Life Science and Biology Vocabulary Journal. Working by yourself or with a partner, use the definitions from pages 62 and 63 of your Work Text to complete the rest of the entry for each word.

carnivore	consumer	decomposer	emphasize	herbivore
nutrient	omnivore	prepare	producer	scavenger

Bodies of Vertebrates and Invertebrates

Read the passage below. Think about the meaning of the words printed in **bold**. Circle any words that start with *endo-* or *exo-*. Remember that *endo-* means *inside* and *exo-* means *outside*. Write what you think each word means next to it. The first one has been done for you.

In or Out?

Vocabulary Strategy

Use familiar prefixes and suffixes to help you understand the meanings of new words.

bones outside

Two useful ways to group animals are according to the kind of skeleton they have and by whether or not they can control their own body temperature.

Many invertebrate animals such as insects and shellfish have (**exoskeletons**). These light shells provide some protection from predators and the sun. They also keep the animal's body moist. Other organisms have **endoskeletons**. This means that they have bones inside their bodies. Some animals don't follow this rule, however. Turtles, for example, have both an exoskeleton and an endoskeleton.

As a rule, mammals and birds are **endothermic**, or warm-blooded. The root *therm* means

heat. These animals are able to keep their own bodies warm. All other living things, including fish, are **exothermic**, or cold-blooded. However, some fish, such as certain sharks, are able to raise their own body temperatures. They are warmer than the water around them. Heating their eyes and brains in this way gives them an advantage over their cold-blooded prey.

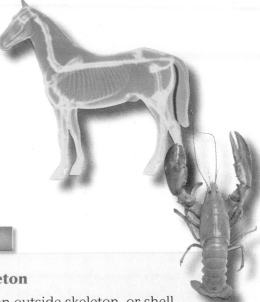

New Life Science and Biology Words

endoskeleton

noun   an inside skeleton

endothermic

adjective   maintains a constant body temperature

exoskeleton

noun   an outside skeleton, or shell

exothermic

adjective   body temperature changes with temperature of surroundings

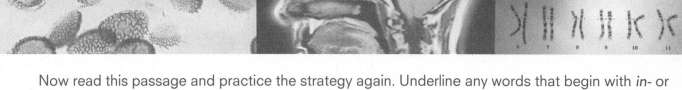

Now read this passage and practice the strategy again. Underline any words that begin with *in-* or end in *–al*. Remember that *in-* means *not* and *–al* names a relationship. Write near each circled word what you think it means.

A Wide World of Invertebrates

We vertebrates might think that having a backbone makes us more important than the worms, ants, and crabs of the world. However, around 95% of the earth's animal species are **invertebrates**. There are between 3 million and 15 million species of invertebrates. There are only 47,000 species of vertebrates.

Perhaps the only thing invertebrates have in common is that they do not have backbones. Some have **segmentation**, with bodies made up of a series of similar parts. Some have **symmetry**. Their body parts are balanced or match in some way. This can be bilateral, or side to side like a butterfly. It can also be radial, or round. You can see this radial symmetry if you look at a **diagram** of a starfish. Other invertebrates, such as sponges and jellyfish, have no symmetry at all.

Metamorphosis also occurs in many invertebrates, especially insects. Vertebrates rarely change shape in this way. Perhaps nothing we vertebrates do will ever equal the drama of a caterpillar becoming a butterfly!

More New Life Science and Biology Words

invertebrate

noun   an animal without a backbone

metamorphosis

noun   the process by which some animals change their form throughout their lives

segmentation

noun   the state of being divided into sections

symmetry

noun   having parts that balance or match one another

See? My brother does have an **exoskeleton**!

Other Useful Words

diagram

noun   a drawing that is used to explain how something looks, what parts it has, or how it works

review

verb   to look over or study something again

Apply the Strategy

Look at a chapter in your textbook that your teacher identifies. Use familiar prefixes and suffixes to help you figure out the meaning of any new words you find.

Finish the Sentence

Use a word from the box to finish each sentence. Write the correct word on the line. Discuss your choices with a partner.

endoskeletons	**endothermic**	**Exothermic**	**diagram**	**metamorphosis**

1 Mammals are _____, or able to keep their own bodies warm.

2 _____ animals cannot control their own body temperatures.

3 When an animal changes from one form to another, it is called _____.

4 Whales, snakes, and donkeys all have _____, or bones inside

their bodies.

5 We had to draw a _____ showing all of the parts of a snail.

exoskeletons	**invertebrates**	**review**	**segments**	**symmetry**

6 You can see the different sections, or _____ on a worm's body.

7 Spiders, snails, insects, and shellfish are called _____ because they do

not have backbones.

8 A butterfly's wings have _____ .

9 Shellfish and insects have _____ that

protect them from predators.

10 It is always a good idea to _____,or look

over your notes before a test.

Word Challenge: Which Word?

With a partner, take turns saying the words listed below. Together, think of a statement for each one that gives a clue about its meaning. Write your statement next to the word. The first one has been done for you.

1 invertebrate *"I have no backbone!"*

2 symmetry _____

3 metamorphosis _____

4 diagram _____

Word Challenge: What's Your Answer?

Take turns with a partner reading each question out loud and writing the answer on the line. Answer the questions in complete sentences. The first one has been done for you.

1 Why might animals with **exoskeletons** grow very slowly? *Animals with exoskeletons grow more slowly because their shells limit how big they can get.*

2 How might **segmentation** help some animals move? _____

_____

3 How does **reviewing** information help you remember it? _____

_____

4 How might an **endothermic** animal heat up its body if it's too cold? _____

_____

Extend the Meaning

Write the letter of the word or phrase that best completes each sentence. Discuss your answers with a partner.

1 An example of **metamorphosis** in animals is _____.
   a. a tadpole changing into a frog
   b. a dog shedding its fur in summer
   c. a child growing taller

2 **Exothermic** animals _____.
   a. do not regulate their own body temperature
   b. have to stay the same temperature all the time
   c. can live at any temperature at all

3 **Symmetry** is _____ among invertebrates.
   a. impossible
   b. common
   c. strange

4 One of the advantages of an **endoskeleton** is that it _____.
   a. gives some protection from the sun
   b. allows an animal to grow more quickly
   c. gives some protection against predators

Word Study: The Prefixes *endo-* and *exo-*

When a prefix *endo-* or *exo-* is added to a root word, it changes the word's meaning.
- *Endo-* means *inside*
- *Exo-* means *outside*

Endo- and *exo-* can be added to many science words.

A. Add the *endo-* and *exo-* prefixes to make new words. Use a dictionary to check your spelling. Do not write in the shaded areas.

		+ *endo-*	+ *exo-*
1	spore		
2	parasite		
3	biology		

B. Write your own definitions for two of the words above. Write your definitions in complete sentences.

1 _____

2 _____

72

The Language of Testing

How would you answer a question like this on a test?

According to the passage, where do most invertebrates live?

    A. in the water
    B. in the air
    C. on the ground
    D. under the ground

 Tip

When a question asks *according to* a person, document, quotation, map, or other source, it is asking what that person or quotation says, or what the map, document, or other source shows.

Test Strategy: If a question asks about something *according to* a person or document, rewrite it by asking what the person or document says or shows. You will probably have to rearrange the sentence.

1 How could you say the question above in a different way?

_____

_____

Try the strategy again by asking these questions in a different way.

2 According to the passage, where is metamorphosis most common?

    A. in reptiles
    B. in birds
    C. in mammals
    D. in insects

3 According to the diagram, where is the symmetry in animals?

    A. between the top and the bottom
    B. between the left and right sides
    C. between the inside and the outside
    D. between the parent and child

_____   _____

_____   _____

_____   _____

 In Your Vocabulary Journal

Find each of these words in your Life Science and Biology Vocabulary Journal. Working by yourself or with a partner, use the definitions from pages 68 and 69 of your Work Text to complete the rest of the entry for each word.

diagram	**endoskeleton**	**endothermic**	**exoskeleton**	**exothermic**
invertebrate	**metamorphosis**	**review**	**segmentation**	**symmetry**

Animal Behavior

Read the passage below. Think about the meanings of the new words printed in **bold**. Underline any definitions that might help you figure out what these words mean. The first one has been done for you.

Threespined Sticklebacks

Vocabulary Strategy

Look for definitions in the text to help you understand the meanings of new words.

Threespined sticklebacks are small fish found in both salt and fresh water. They are known for their interesting **behavior**. Behavior is <u>the way they act</u>.

In mating season, a male stickleback chooses a spot for breeding and becomes highly **territorial**. In other words, it drives off other males to protect its territory. It then makes a mound out of bits of weed, and forms a tunnel inside the mound.

The male stickleback also changes color. Its belly becomes bright orange. This is a form of **communication**, or a way to share information. The fish's orange belly helps it attract females.

When the male sees a female, he dances in a zig-zag to get the female to come into the tunnel. The male does this dance because of **instinct**. No one has taught him how to do it. When the female is in the tunnel, she will lay her eggs. The male fertilizes the eggs once they are laid. He also guards them until they hatch.

New Life Science and Biology Words

behavior
  noun   the way an organism acts

communicate
  verb   to share information

instinct
  noun   something that people and animals do naturally without having to learn it

territorial
  adjective   describes an animal that is protective of a certain area

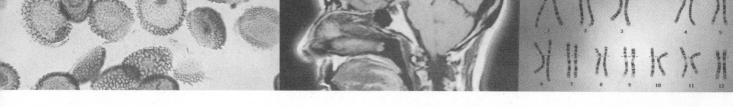

Now read this passage and practice the vocabulary strategy again. Underline any definitions in the passage that can help you figure out what the new words in **bold** mean.

Whooping Cranes

Whooping cranes are one of the rarest birds in North America. In 1939 there were only 18 left. Today, there are still fewer than 200 in the wild.

Young cranes have several **predators**, or animals that kill other animals for food. In addition, adult cranes are **prey** for bobcats. An animal that is killed for food by another animal is called prey. The main threat for cranes, however, is loss of habitat.

Whooping cranes do not **hibernate**, or sleep through the winter. Instead, they migrate from northern Canada to the Gulf coast of Texas. The trip is hard, and many cranes die along the way.

Programs to breed whooping cranes have been slightly successful. There are a few problems, however. The young birds **imprint**, or form a strong relationship with a parent. If the birds imprint on humans, they can never go back into the wild. Some scientists **formulated** a plan to solve the problem. All humans who work with the cranes wear clothes that make them look like cranes. The cranes are also taught to migrate by following a very small plane.

More New Life Science and Biology Words

hibernate

verb   to spend a long period of time, usually in winter, sleeping or resting

imprint

verb   to form a strong relationship with a parent figure

predator

noun   an animal that kills other animals and eats them

prey

noun   an animal that is killed for food by another animal

"Kenny is very **territorial**."

Other Useful Words

debate

noun   a discussion about two sides of an issue or idea

verb   to discuss two sides of an issue or idea

formulate

verb   to develop an idea or plan

Apply the Strategy

Look at a chapter in your textbook that your teacher identifies. Use definitions in the text to help you figure out the meaning of any new words you find.

Matching

Finish the sentences in Group A with words from Group B. Write the letter of the word on the line. Discuss your choices with a partner.

Group A

Group B

1 Young fish are easy _____ for predators.

A. territorial

2 Birds are not taught how to build nests. They do it by _____.

B. communicate

C. prey

D. debated

3 Animals use sound, touch, and smell to _____.

E. instinct

4 Birds are often _____ when they are protecting a nest.

5 Our class discussed, or _____ all of the sides to the argument.

Group A

Group B

6 A baby bird will _____ or form a strong relationship with the first moving object it sees after it hatches.

F. behavior

G. formulate

H. hibernate

7 We had to _____, or develop a plan for our class project.

I. imprint

J. predator

8 Some animals _____ through the coldest months of winter.

9 A spider traps other insects to eat, so it is called a _____.

10 Some animal _____ is learned, and some comes from instinct.

Word Challenge: Correct or Incorrect

Read the sentences below either with a partner or by yourself. Write **C** if the sentence is correct, and write **I** if the sentence is incorrect. Rewrite the incorrect sentences. The first one has been done for you.

1 ___I___ Snakes eat mice and other small **predators**.

   Snakes eat mice and other small prey.

2 _____ The **behavior** of the two male bears was fascinating to watch.

   _____

3 _____ Owls snatch up their **prey** with their claws.

   _____

4 _____ People on both sides of the **debate** agreed on what should be done.

   _____

Word Challenge: What's Your Reason?

Take turns with a partner reading the statements below out loud. Think of a reason for each statement and write it on the line. Write your reasons in complete sentences.

1 Why do animals **hibernate**? _They hibernate so they don't_

   have to find food in the winter.

2 Why do animals need to **communicate** with each other? _____

   _____

3 Why is it good for babies to **imprint** with a parent? _____

   _____

4 Why are some animals **territorial**? _____

   _____

Word Pairs

Choose the pair of words from each group that best completes each sentence. Write the words on the lines. Discuss your choices with a partner.

1 Even a _____ can be _____ to a larger animal.

territorial   prey   predator   communicate

2 _____ makes the newly hatched ducklings _____ on the first moving object they see.

hibernate   debate   Instinct   imprint

3 Snails are not taught how to _____ in winter, but they do it by

_____.

instinct   hibernate   imprint   behavior

4 Song birds _____ with each other to warn of _____ nearby.

imprint   predators   prey   communicate

Word Study: The Suffix -al

When the suffix -al is added to a noun such as *behavior*, it does two things:

- First, it makes the noun an adjective: *behavioral*.
- Second, it adds "related to" to the word's meaning.

You may need to change or add a vowel at the end of a word before adding -al: *instinct* + -al = *instinctual.*

Add -al to each noun to make a new word. Write a definition for each word. Use a dictionary to check your spelling and definitions.

		+ -al	Definition
1	**behavior**		
2	**instinct**		
3	**predator**		
4	**territory**		

The Language of Testing

How would you answer a question like this on a test?

Based on the passage, which animal is the most aggressive?

    A. the squirrel
    B. the chipmunk
    C. the groundhog
    D. the opossum

 Tip

When you see the words *based on* in a question, it means that you need to look at a map, chart, or picture to answer the question.

Test Strategy: If a question has the phrase *based on* in it, rewrite it to ask you to look at the chart, table, map, or picture to find out the information you need to answer the question.

1 How could you say the question above in a different way?

_____

_____

Try the strategy again by asking these questions in a different way.

2 Based on the diagram, what is the favorite food of voles?

    A. grasses
    B. acorns
    C. worms
    D. berries

3 Based on the information in the passage, what ways can animals communicate?

    A. through smell
    B. through touch
    C. through sound
    D. all of the above

_____   _____

_____   _____

_____   _____

 ## In Your Vocabulary Journal

Find each of these words in your Life Science and Biology Vocabulary Journal. Working by yourself or with a partner, use the definitions from pages 74 and 75 of your Work Text to complete the rest of the entry for each word.

behavior	**communicate**	**debate**	**formulate**	**hibernate**
imprint	**instinct**	**predator**	**prey**	**territorial**

Lesson 14

Human and Animal Systems

Read the passage below. Think about the meanings of the words printed in **bold**. Create associations between words you know and the new words. These will help you remember what the new words mean. Mark or write these associations near the new words in the passage. The first one has been done for you.

breathing

Vocabulary Strategy

Create associations between things you know and the new words to "anchor" your understanding of new words. You can complete a Word Anchor chart to help you create associations.

Smoking and Your Body

Everyone knows that smoking is bad for you. What is amazing is how many body systems smoking can harm. It makes sense that smoking hurts **respiration** and the respiratory system. For example, smokers are more likely to suffer not just constant coughing and wheezing, but more serious illnesses as well.

Smokers also suffer from diseases connected to blood **circulation** and the circulatory system such as heart disease and stroke. The materials in cigarettes harm veins and cause the blood to be less able to carry oxygen.

Smokers can get many forms of cancer, especially lung cancer. They are also more likely to catch colds and the flu. This is probably because their **immune** systems do not work as well as those of non-smokers.

Smoking also harms **reproduction**. Smoking can cause problems for both the baby and the mother. It can sometimes even cause a baby to die before it is born. A pregnant woman smoking a cigarette is **equivalent** to her baby smoking a cigarette.

There is some good news, though. You can avoid many of these health risks by not smoking. It is that simple.

No Smoking

New Life Science and Biology Words

circulation

   noun   the movement of blood through the body

immune

   adjective   being protected from or being able to fight off certain diseases

reproduction

   noun   the process plants and animals use to create offspring

respiration

   noun   the process of breathing

Now read this passage and practice the vocabulary strategy again. Write or mark near the new words in the passage any associations you can use to anchor the meaning of the new words.

Health Through Nutrition, or, You Are What You Eat

Your body depends on what you consume for its nutritional and energy needs. How can you get or stay healthy through diet? Let's take a look.

Your **skeletal** system includes teeth and bones. To keep bones and teeth healthy and strong, you should eat plenty of calcium. You can find calcium in dairy products such as milk and cheese, in green leafy vegetables, and in tofu. The muscles in your **muscular** system need carbohydrates and proteins. Carbohydrates are sugars found in pasta and bread. Protein is good for growth.

Even your **digestion** can be boosted by proper diet. Plenty of fiber keeps your digestive system working smoothly. "Good" bacteria, such as those found in yogurt, aid digestion.

Your **sensory** system also will not work well if you are not getting all of the nutrients you need. For example, vitamin A, which is found in carrots, helps with healthy eyesight. You can **inquire**, or ask for more information about nutrition from your doctor.

More New Life Science and Biology Words

digestion

   noun   the way in which animals and humans take in nutrients from food and pass waste

muscular

   adjective   having to do with muscles

sensory

   adjective   having to do with the five senses

skeletal

   adjective   having to do with an animal's skeleton

"The city's bad **circulation** is harming your **respiration**."

Other Useful Words

equivalent

   adjective   equal or very similar

inquire

   verb   to ask a question or investigate

Apply the Strategy

Look at a chapter in your textbook that your teacher identifies. Use associations in the text to help you figure out the meaning of any new words you find.

Finish the Paragraph

Use the words in the box to finish the paragraph below. Write the correct word in the blank. One word will not be used. Discuss your choices with a partner.

circulation	digestion	immune	muscular
inquire	respiration	sensory	skeletal

Both your coach and your doctor will be pleased if you decide to exercise more. Yes,

your _____ **1** system will improve with increased muscle strength and

flexibility, but other body systems will benefit, too. Bones in the _____ **2**

system get stronger with exercise. The ability of the _____ **3** system to

fight disease improves. During exercise, when you are breathing heavily, your

_____ **4** rate goes up. Exercise increases _____ **5** of

blood in the body, and lowers the risk of heart disease. While exercise may not directly

affect _____ **6** and the absorption of nutrients, it does help prevent and

fight obesity, or becoming overweight. Next time you

see your doctor, _____ **7** about

the amount of exercise that is right for you.

82

Word Challenge: True or False

Take turns with a partner reading the sentences below out loud. Write **T** next to each sentence that is true. Write **F** next to each sentence that is false. Rewrite the false sentences. The first one has been done for you.

1 _T_ The **circulation** of blood happens in arteries and veins.

2 ____ **Digestion** is the process through which animals take up oxygen.

_____

3 ____ Our **immune** systems help protect us from disease.

_____

4 ____ The **muscular** system includes muscles and bones.

_____

5 ____ Things that are **equivalent** are nothing alike.

_____

Word Challenge: Which Word?

With a partner, take turns saying the words listed below. Together, think of a statement for each that gives a clue about its meaning. Write your statement next to the word. The first one has been done for you.

1 reproduction _"I 'm how animals make more animals."_

2 sensory _____

3 skeletal _____

4 respiration _____

5 inquire _____

Word Connections

In the spaces at the top of the wheel, write the words from the box that connect to the center word or idea. In the shaded spaces at the bottom of the wheel, write the words that do not connect. Discuss your choices with a partner.

blood	digestion	muscles	veins	lungs	bones

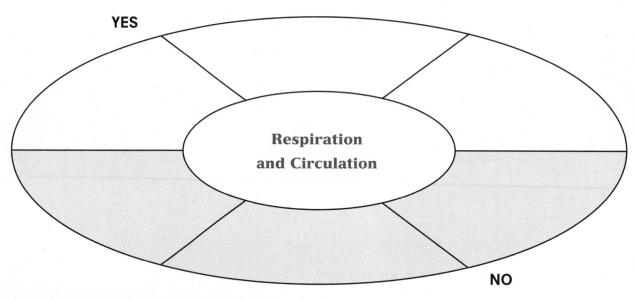

Word Study: The Suffix -ive

When the suffix -ive is added to a root verb such as *digest*, it changes the verb's meaning:

- First, it changes the verb to a noun or an adjective: *digestive*.
- Second, it adds the meaning "belonging to" to the word.

> You may need to change, drop, or add letters to the ending before adding -ive.
>
> **sense** (v.) to know by hearing, feeling, seeing, smelling, or tasting
> **sensitive** (adj.) able to sense strongly

Add the suffix –ive to the words below. Write your own definition for each. Use a dictionary to check your spelling and definitions.

	+ –ive	Definition
1 reproduce		
2 digest		
3 adapt		
4 instinct		

The Language of Testing

How would you answer a question like this on a test?

"Your immune system is your first defense against disease." What does this statement **illustrate**?

    A. The immune system fights disease.
    B. The immune system can fight all diseases.
    C. The immune system helps us absorb nutrients.
    D. The immune system needs medicines.

Tip

The word *illustrate* means *show* or *explain*.

Test Strategy: If you see a question that asks what a statement, chart, graph, or picture *illustrates*, rewrite it to ask what the statement, chart, graph or picture *means* or *shows*.

1 How could you say the question above in a different way?

_____

_____

Try the strategy again by asking these questions in a different way.

2 What does the chart illustrate about the number of species threatened by extinction?

    A. It has gotten smaller.
    B. It has remained the same.
    C. It has increased.
    D. It is not possible to tell.

_____

_____

_____

3 What does the map illustrate about the U.S. nesting grounds of sandhill cranes?

    A. They nest only in the South.
    B. They nest only in the North.
    C. They nest only in the East.
    D. They nest only in the West.

_____

_____

_____

In Your Vocabulary Journal

Find each of these words in your Life Science and Biology Vocabulary Journal. Working by yourself or with a partner, use the definitions from pages 80 and 81 of your Work Text to complete the rest of the entry for each word.

circulation	digestion	equivalent	immune	inquire
muscular	reproduction	respiration	sensory	skeletal

Lesson 15

Reproduction and Growth

Read the passage below. Think about the meanings of the words printed in **bold**. Underline any synonyms for the new words. Draw an arrow from each to the bold word it describes. The first one has been done for you.

Life Stages

Vocabulary Strategy

Use synonyms to help you understand the meaning of new words. Look for clues in the text, like *or*, to help you find synonyms.

All animals go through stages in their lives. Although they all go through a process of <u>change and growth</u>, or **development**, it is slightly different for every species. An early life stage for an animal is the **embryo** stage. This stage begins with fertilization. The tiny group of cells that form the embryo grows rapidly. At first, all of the cells look alike, but they develop into different types of cells. Those cells might become skin cells, nerve cells, muscle cells, or cells that form tissues and organs.

When a very young animal is first born or hatched, it is called an **infant**, or baby. Infants develop rapidly. They are constantly growing and changing, moving toward being an adult. Between infant and adult, the animal becomes an **adolescent**. Adolescents have many things in common with adults, but are not fully grown. Adult animals continue to change as they age.

Each animal develops in its own special way. That's because each animal has a slightly different genetic make up from all other animals. It is that genetic difference that makes you the unique person you are!

New Life Science and Biology Words

adolescent

noun a young animal that is developing into an adult

development

noun the process of growing or changing

embryo

noun the earliest growth of an organism, when there are a limited number of similar cells

infant

noun a baby or very young animal

Now read this passage and practice the vocabulary strategy again. Underline any synonyms and draw an arrow from each one to the new word it describes.

 ## Up Until Birth

Every living organism reproduces. There is some sort of natural instinct, drive, or need in an organism to **propagate** and create more of its species. The basics of sexual reproduction for most plants and animals are similar. An egg is produced in the female **ovary**. The egg joins with a male reproductive cell, and an embryo is formed. At this point, the development process differs among various species. Let's follow the **series** of events for a mammal.

As the embryo develops, it attaches itself inside the female or mother. At that point, the female is considered to be **pregnant**. The offspring is developing inside her body. While the female is pregnant, her body releases various **hormones**. These chemicals help the mother's body provide a good environment for the growing offspring.

The embryo's cells quickly start to become different from one another. The embryo changes and grows into a fetus. Cells in the fetus continue to divide and change. All the organs, tissues, and body parts develop. When the fetus is able to maintain life outside the mother, it goes through the process of birth. A new infant is born!

 ## More New Life Science and Biology Words

hormone

noun   a chemical made by an organism that produces a special effect in certain cells

ovary

noun   a female organ that produces eggs

pregnant

adjective   describes a female animal with offspring developing inside of her body

propagate

verb   to produce offspring

She's 14 hours old and thinks she's an **adolescent**.

 ## Other Useful Words

infer

noun   to guess or come to a conclusion based on facts or knowledge

series

noun   a number of things or events that come in a certain order

Apply the Strategy

Look at a chapter in your class textbook that your teacher identifies. Use synonyms in the text to help you figure out the meaning of any new words you find.

The Right Word

Read each sentence. Look at the word or phrase that is underlined. Write a word from the box that means the same or almost the same as the underlined word or phrase. Discuss your answers with a partner.

adolescents	development	hormones	ovaries	propagate

1 _____ Plants <u>produce offspring</u> differently than animals.

2 _____ It is amazing to watch the rapid <u>process of growing and changing</u> babies go through during their first year of life.

3 _____ As we go through different stages of life, the levels of different <u>chemicals that affect cells</u> in our bodies change.

4 _____ Our veterinarian told us that our retriever couldn't have puppies because of a problem in her <u>female reproductive organs</u>.

5 _____ The arena was filled with screaming <u>young humans</u>, who were excited to see their favorite band play.

embryo	infer	infants	series	pregnant

6 _____ Along with a number of toddlers, there were three young <u>babies</u> at the daycare center.

7 _____ We could tell that our cat was <u>developing babies inside</u> because her belly grew much larger.

8 _____ Based on the information we had, we could <u>come to a conclusion</u> that our teacher was unhappy with our grades on the test.

9 _____ Under the microscope we could see that the <u>early growth stage of an organism</u> had a few cells that all looked alike.

10 _____ For our project, we drew a <u>number of pictures in order</u> showing the life cycle of a chicken.

Word Challenge: Finish the Idea

With a partner, take turns reading the incomplete sentences below. Write an ending for each. The first one has been done for you.

1 A **series** of pictures showing my day so far would have _me eating breakfast, riding the bus to school, and sitting in this class._

2 When the **hormones** were released, the cell changed because _____

3 Organisms **propagate** because _____

4 In order to reproduce, the female **ovary** must produce eggs because _____

Word Challenge: What's Your Answer?

Take turns with a partner reading each question out loud and writing an answer on the line. Answer the questions in complete sentences. The first one has been done for you.

1 What does an **infant** look like? _An infant is small, with a big head and little arms and legs._

2 Describe the stage of human **development** you are in. _____

3 What are two characteristics of an **infant**? _____

4 What could you **infer** if everyone at school was wearing their pajamas? _____

_____

Synonyms and Antonyms

Write a synonym or an antonym for the vocabulary words below. In some cases, you might be able to provide both. Discuss your answers with a partner.

		Synonym	Antonym
1	development		
2	infant		
3	series		
4	infer		
5	propagate		

Word Study: The Prefixes *pre-* and *post-*

Pre- and *post-* are often added to words that name an event or period of time.
- When the prefix *pre-* is added to a word, it adds *before* to the word's meaning.

- When the prefix *post-* is added to a word, it adds *after* to the word's meaning.

A. Add the prefixes *pre-* and *post-* to make new words.

		+ *pre-*	+ *post-*
1	adolescent		
2	infant		
3	pregnancy		

B. Fill each blank with a *pre-* word or *post-* word from the chart.

1 A person's body changes when they become an adolescent. The stage before that happens is called the _____ stage.

2 After giving birth, a woman is no longer pregnant. The period after giving birth is the _____ period.

The Language of Testing

How would you answer a question like this on a test?

What was the result when hormones were released in the body?

    A. Some cells changed their normal activity.
    B. All cells changed their normal activity.
    C. Some cells began to divide more rapidly.
    D. The adolescent became an adult.

 Tip

The phrase *what was the result when* can also mean *what happened after* or *what happened next.*

Test Strategy: If you see a question that uses the phrase *what was the result when*, rewrite it using the phrases *what happened after* or *what happened next.*

1 How could you say the question above in a different way?

_____

_____

Try the strategy again by asking these questions in a different way.

2 What was the result when the egg was fertilized?

    A. An infant was formed.
    B. An embryo was formed.
    C. An adult developed.
    D. An adolescent developed.

3 What was the result when normal development was interrupted?

    A. The organism died.
    B. The organism became a mutant.
    C. The organism developed more slowly than usual.
    D. There was no change.

_____   _____

_____   _____

_____   _____

 In Your Vocabulary Journal

Find each of these words in your Life Science and Biology Vocabulary Journal. Working by yourself or with a partner, use the definitions from pages 86 and 87 in your Work Text to complete the rest of the entry for each word.

adolescent	development	embryo	hormone	infant
infer	ovary	pregnant	propagate	series

Glossary

Aa

according (to) (uh **kawr** dihng)

preposition as someone has said or written (***According** to the encyclopedia, there are many different kinds of bacteria.*)

acquire (uh **kweyer**)

verb to get or receive something new (*Over the centuries, many plants and animals have **acquired** new characteristics to help them survive.*)

adaptation (a dap **tay** shuhn)

noun the process of changing, or a change that has been made (***Adaptation** has allowed many plants and animals to survive in a changing environment.*)

adolescent (ad uh **lehs** uhnt)

noun a young animal that is developing into an adult (*Our dog is about two years old and is really an **adolescent**.*)

advantage (uhd **van** tihj)

noun a helpful trait or characteristic that others may not have (*By camping near the spring, we had the **advantage** of having fresh water to drink.*)

algae (**al** guh)

noun very simple plants that grow in water and have no leaves or roots (*Because of all the **algae**, the water looked very cloudy.*)

analyze (**an** uh leyez)

verb to study information (*After **analyzing** the data, the scientists found that the animals were the same age.*)

assemble (uh **sehm** buhl)

verb to put parts together (*Our assignment was to **assemble** a display of different kinds of seeds.*)

Bb

bacteria (bak **tihr** ee uh)

noun one-celled organisms that live in air, soil, water, animals, and plants (*Many types of **bacteria** cause diseases in both plants and animals.*)

behavior (bih **hay** vyuhr)

noun the way an organism acts (*We studied the **behavior** of one-celled organisms and how they responded to light.*)

biosphere (**by** uh sfihr)

noun Earth's land and air where life can exist (*Earth's **biosphere** supports many kinds of plant and animal life.*)

botany (**bah** tuhn ee)

noun the study of plants (*About half of our Life Science class time was spent on **botany**.*)

Cc

calculate (**cal** kyuh layt)

verb to add, subtract, multiply, or divide numbers (*The teacher had us **calculate** probability by flipping coins.*)

carnivore (**kahr** nuh vohr)

noun an organism that eats mostly meat (*Lions and wolves are **carnivores**.*)

cellular (**sel** yuh luhr)

adjective having to do with cells, the smallest unit of life (*The doctor discovered a disease at the **cellular** level.*)

chlorophyll (**klohr** uh fihl)

noun the material in a plant that makes it green (***Chlorophyll** in plants' leaves helps convert light into energy.*)

chromosome (**kroh** muh sohm)

> *noun*   part of a cell that holds all of the cell's information (*Your* **chromosomes** *contain information about your eye and hair color.*)

circulation (suhr kyuh **lay** shuhn)

> *noun*   the movement of blood through the body (*When we studied the circulatory system, we learned about the* **circulation** *of blood.*)

classification (**kla** suh fuh kay shuhn)

> *noun*   a way of grouping things based on their similarities (*The* **classification** *of plants and animals is an ongoing process.*)

communicate (kuh myoo nuh **kayt**)

> *verb*   to share information (*Bees can* **communicate** *the location of flowers through a series of motions, somewhat like a dance.*)

competition (kahm puh **tih** shuhn)

> *noun*   the act of trying to succeed over someone or something (**Competition** *for food drove many animals to migrate to other areas.*)

conclude (kuhn **klood**)

> *verb*   to make a final decision based on facts or observations (*From this experiment, we can* **conclude** *that water boils at 100°C.*)

confirm (**kuhn** fuhrm)

> *verb*   to prove that something is true (*We were able to* **confirm** *that the flight was leaving at 10:03 tomorrow morning.*)

consult (kuhn **suhlt**)

> *verb*   to ask or check for information or advice (*Nora had to* **consult** *a dictionary to find out how to spell chlorophyll.*)

consumer (kuhn **soom** uhr)

> *noun*   an organism that eats or uses up something (*Humans are considered* **consumers** *because we eat plants and meat and use natural resources.*)

cultivate (**kuhl** tuh vayt)

> *verb*   to make the ground ready to grow crops or to grow crops (*Farmers* **cultivate** *their fields in order to raise corn, wheat, and oats.*)

> *verb*   to develop something that could be good for you (*Scientists* **cultivated** *a drug improved the immune system.)*

Dd

data (**day** tuh)

> *noun*   information, facts, or numbers gathered for a purpose (*The experiment gathered* **data** *about comets.*)

debate (dih **bayt**)

> *noun*   a discussion about two sides of an issue or idea. (*We held a* **debate** *about the pros and cons of recycling.*)

> *verb*   to discuss two sides of an issue or idea (*We were asked to* **debate** *about genetic research.*)

decomposer (dee kuhm **poh** zuhr)

> *noun*   an organism that helps break down dead matter (*Many bacteria and fungi are classified as* **decomposers**.*)

define (dih **feyen**)

> *verb*   to describe or explain something completely (*His report* **defined** *the characteristics of the bald eagle.*)

demonstrate (**deh** muhn strayt)

> *noun*   to show (*Jorge* **demonstrated** *how to use a microscope properly.*)

development (dih **veh** luhp muhnt)

> *noun*   the process of growing or changing (*We could watch the horse's* **development** *from year to year.*)

diagram (**dy** uh gram)

　　noun　a drawing that is used to explain how something looks, what parts it has, or how it works (*Mrs. Gomez drew a* **diagram** *that showed the parts of the heart.*)

diffusion (dih **fyoo** juhn)

　　noun　the process in which very small pieces of something move from where there are many to where there are fewer (*Because of* **diffusion** *we could smell her perfume all over the room.*)

digestion (dy **jehs** chuhn)

　　noun　the way in which animals and humans take in nutrients from food and pass waste (*The first step in* **digestion** *begins with chewing your food.*)

disorder (dih **sawr** duhr)

　　noun　an illness, fault, or problem (*The* **disorder** *caused her to limp on her left leg.*)

distinguish (dih **sting** gwish)

　　verb　to be able to tell the difference between or among two or more things (*He could* **distinguish** *between a poisonous and nonpoisonous spider.*)

diversity (duh **vuhr** suh tee)

　　noun　the amount of difference among things that are otherwise mostly alike (*The* **diversity** *of flowers in the garden was beautiful.*)

dominant (**dah** muh nuhnt)

　　adjective　stronger or more noticeable (*I'm left-handed, so my left hand is* **dominant**.)

Ee

ecosystem (**ee** koh sihs tuhm)

　　noun　the relationship between organisms and their environment (*The wetlands around the Chesapeake Bay is a unique* **ecosystem**.)

ecology (ih **kah** luh jee)

　　noun　the study of living things and their environment (*The* **ecology** *of the desert centers around the lack of water.*)

embryo (**ehm** bree oh)

　　noun　the earliest growth of an organism, when there are a limited number of similar cells (*The chicken* **embryos** *developed inside the eggs.*)

emphasize (**ehm** fuh syz)

　　verb　to show that something is important (*He* **emphasized** *the need for people to use natural resources wisely.*)

endoskeleton (ehn doh **skeh** luh tuhn)

　　noun　an inside skeleton (*Mammals have* **endoskeletons**, *which are an inner framework.*)

endothermic (ehn duh **thur** mihk)

　　adjective　maintains a constant body temperature (*Monkeys are* **endothermic** *animals.*)

equilibrium (ee kwuh **lih** bree uhm)

　　noun　a balance between two or more forces or things (*The Eustachian tube, which runs between the middle ear and the throat, helps maintain an* **equilibrium** *of air pressure in the ear.*)

equivalent (ih **kwih** vuh luhnt)

　　adjective　equal or very similar (*I found a coat that was* **equivalent** *to the one I lost.*)

estimate (**ehs** tuh mut)

　　verb　to guess at the amount of something (*We* **estimated** *that we made almost $500 from the bake sale.*)

　　noun　a guess at the amount of something (*The builder gave an* **estimate** *of $8,000 for the work.*)

evaluate (ih **val** yuh wayt)

　　verb　to determine something's value or importance (*We had to* **evaluate** *the importance of the project.*)

evolution (eh vuh **loo** shuhn)

noun the process by which plants and animals develop and change over millions of years *(The theory of **evolution** emerged in the 19th century.)*

exoskeleton (ehk soh **skeh** luh tuhn)

noun an outside skeleton, or shell *(Insects, such as grasshoppers, have an **exoskeleton**.)*

exothermic (ehk soh **thur** mihk)

adjective body temperature changes with temperature of surroundings *(Snakes and other reptiles are **exothermic** animals.)*

extinct (ik **stihngkt**)

adjective having to do with a species that is no longer alive *(The dodo, a large bird, is now **extinct**.)*

Ff

factor (**fak** tuhr)

noun something that causes a result or outcome *(Chicago's location on Lake Michigan is one of the **factors** that made it a trading center in the 19th century.)*

fermentation (fur mun **tay** shun)

noun a process that produces energy without using oxygen *(Your muscles get sore after a work-out because of **fermentation** in the cells.)*

fertilize (**fuhr** tuhl yz)

verb to make soil richer so that plants will grow better, or to bring together an egg with the male reproductive cell to reproduce offspring *(Many people **fertilize** their gardens in the early spring before planting.)*

fission (**fih** juhn)

noun making a new organism by splitting apart *(Amoebas reproduce through **fission**.)*

focus (**foh** kuhs)

verb to examine closely or to concentrate on *(She **focused** her attention on how to set up the experiment.)*

noun the center of activity or attention *(The **focus** of the conference was viral diseases.)*

formulate (**fawr** myoo layt)

verb to develop an idea or plan *(We had to **formulate** a plan for our science project.)*

fossil (**fah** suhl)

noun remains of a dead plant or animal that have been preserved in stone *(We found a **fossil** of a leaf in the rocks down by the riverbank.)*

function (**fuhnk** shuhn)

noun the purpose of something *(The heart's **function** is to pump blood.)*

fungus (**fuhng** guhs)

noun an organism that is like a plant but does not have leaves, seeds, or flowers *(Mushrooms are one kind of **fungus**.)*

Gg

generation (jeh nuh **ray** shuhn)

noun all the living things around the same age *(The last **generation** of plants had mostly blue flowers.)*

genetic (juh **neh** tihk)

adjective having to do with the way features are passed from one organism to another *(DNA is the **genetic** material in cells.)*

germinate (**juhr** muh nayt)

verb to begin to grow from a seed *(The seeds began to **germinate** about four days after they were planted.)*

Hh

habitat (**ha** buh tat)
    noun the place where a plant or animal usually lives and grows (*Much of the tiger's natural* **habitat** *is gone.*)

herbivore (**uhr** buh vohr
    noun an organism that eats mostly plants (*Vegetarians are* **herbivores**.)

heredity (huh **reh** duh tee)
    noun the way in which features are passed from a parent to offspring (*Because of* **heredity**, *almost everyone in the family has blonde hair.*)

hibernate (**hy** buhr nayt)
    verb to spend a long period of time, usually winter, sleeping or resting (*Before they* **hibernate**, *bears eat a lot of food.*)

homeostasis (hoh mee oh **sta** sis)
    noun the balance that living things keep in their bodies (*Through* **homeostasis**, *human beings have an internal temperature of 98.6° F.*)

hormone (**hawr** mohn)
    noun a chemical made by an organism that produces a special effect in certain cells (*After the deer gave birth to the fawn, there was a change in the level of the doe's* **hormones**.)

host (**hohst**)
    noun an organism that is home to another form of life, or someone who serves or entertains guests (*Many types of animals are* **hosts** *to various parasites such as worms.*)

    verb to serve or entertain guests, or to be home for another organism (*Victoria* **hosted** *a Halloween costume party.*)

hybrid (**heye** bruhd)
    noun the offspring of two different species that has features of both (*The corn was a* **hybrid** *variety that made it grow well in the sandy soil.*)

hypothesis (hy **pahth** uh sihs)
    noun a guess or an idea that can be tested (*Her* **hypothesis** *about the depth of the topsoil was correct.*)

Ii

immune (ih **myoon**)
    adjective being protected from or being able to fight off certain diseases (*After I had measles, I was* **immune** *to them in the future.*)

imprint (im **print**)
    verb to form a strong relationship with a parent figure (*Some ducks* **imprint** *with other animals.*)

indicate (**ihn** duh kayt)
    verb to point out or point to something (*Please* **indicate** *which plant you would like to plant over there.*)

infant (**ihn** fuhnt)
    noun a baby or very young animal (*We looked through the window and saw all the new-born* **infants**.)

infer (ihn **fuhr**)
    noun to guess or come to a conclusion based on facts or knowledge (*These plants grew poorly when there was little light, so we can* **infer** *they need more light to grow well.*)

inherit (ihn **hehr** uht)
    verb to receive something from a parent or grandparent (*Emily* **inherited** *her mother's long fingers.*)

inquire (ihn **kwyr**)
    verb to ask a question or investigate (*We went to the store to* **inquire** *about the prices for MP3 players.*)

instinct (**ihn** stihng kt)
    noun something that people and animals do naturally without having to learn it (*My dog's hunting* **instincts** *are very strong.*)

interaction (ihn tuhr **ak** shuhn)

> *noun* the way in which two or more things affect one another (*The **interaction** between my dog and cat is very interesting to watch.*)

interpret (ihn **tuhr** pruht)

> *verb* to decide the meaning of something and explain it (*Jamal was asked to **interpret** the marks on the cave wall.*)

invertebrate (ihn **vuhr** tuh bruht)

> *noun* an animal without a back bone (*All forms of jellyfish are **invertebrates**.*)

investigation (in vest uh **gay** shuhn)

> *noun* an organized plan for gathering information about something (*The **investigation** required them to gather plants from all over the world.*)

Kk

kingdom (**kihng** duhm)

> *noun* the top level of scientific classification (*All birds are part of the animal **kingdom**.*)

Mm

membrane (**mehm** brayn)

> *noun* the thin, outer layer of a cell or a thin, flexible sheet of skin (*Some liquids can pass through the cell **membrane**.*)

metabolism (muh **tab** uh lih zum)

> *noun* the way a living thing changes food into energy (*The rate of **metabolism** varies from person to person.*)

metamorphosis (meh tuh **mawr** fuh suhs)

> *noun* the process by which some animals change their form throughout their lives (*We watched the caterpillar go through **metamorphosis** and turn into a butterfly.*)

mitosis (meye **toh** sis)

> *noun* the process in which a cell divides into two (*We learned how cells divide through **mitosis**.*)

mold (**mohld**)

> *noun* an organism that grows on rotting food or other warm, slightly wet objects (*The old loaf of bread was covered in a blue gray **mold**.*)

muscular (**muhs** kyuh luhr)

> *adjective* having to do with muscles (*The body's **muscular** system helps us move and breathe.*)

mutation (myoo **tay** shuhn)

> *noun* a sudden change in a plant or animal to a new kind of plant or animal (***Mutation** happens quickly in bacteria, which allows it to adapt to its environment.*)

Nn

niche (**nihch**)

> *noun* a certain place or position occupied by an organism (*Termites fill a special **niche** by breaking down plant fibers.*)

nucleus (**noo** klee uhs)

> *noun* the central part of a cell that controls what it does (*The cell's **nucleus** controlled the growth of the cell.*)

nutrient (**noo** tree uhnt)

> *noun* a substance that a plant or animal needs to help it live and grow (*Fresh fruits contain many healthy **nutrients**.*)

Oo

observation (ahb suhr **vay** shuhn)

> *noun* the act of carefully watching something to gather information about it (*Through their **observation**, they discovered a new type of beetle.*)

omnivore (**ahm** nih vohr)

> *noun* an organism that eats both plants and meat (*Most of the people I know are **omnivores**.*)

order (**awr** duhr)

    noun the way things are placed or organized, or a level of scientific classification (*Moles are in the **order** insectavora because they eat insects.*)

organ (**awr** gun)

    noun a part of an animal that does a specific job (*The heart, kidneys, and liver are all **organs** in the human body.*)

organism (**awr** guh nih zuhm

    noun a plant, animal, or single-celled life form (*We watched the tiny **organisms** under the microscope.*)

origin (**awr** uh juhn)

    noun the beginning or source of something (*The **origin** of the Mississippi River is in northern Minnesota.*)

ovary (**oh** vuh ree)

    noun a female organ that produces eggs (*Most female animals have two **ovaries** that produce egg cells.*)

Pp

parasite (**par** uh syt)

    noun an organism that lives on or in another organism and feeds on it (*Sasha got a **parasite** that made her sick because she drank some dirty water.*)

pedigree (**peh** duh gree)

    noun a chart or list of all of the ancestors of an offspring (*The dog's breeder said its **pedigree** included many grand champion show dogs.*)

phase (**fayz**)

    noun one step or stage in a process (*There are many **phases** of mitosis.*)

photosynthesis (foh toh **sihn** thuh suhs)

    noun the process by which a plant makes food by using sunlight and air (*Plants make much of their own food through **photosynthesis**.*)

pigment (**pihg** muhnt)

    noun a material that gives something color (*Chlorophyll has a green **pigment** in it.*)

pollination (pah luh **nay** shuhn)

    noun the process of moving pollen from the male part of a plant to a female part of a plant (*Honey bees carry pollen on their bodies from one plant to the next, an important step in **pollination**.*)

predator (**preh** duh tuhr)

    noun an animal that kills other animals and eats them (*Many types of birds, such as eagles and hawks, are **predators**.*)

predict (prih **dihkt**)

    verb to guess what will happen (*The meteorologist **predicted** that it will rain every day this week.*)

pregnant (**prehg** nuhnt)

    adjective describes a female animal with offspring developing inside of her body (*The **pregnant** woman was going to have her baby next month.*)

prepare (prih **pehr**)

    verb to get ready for something ahead of time (*Make sure you **prepare** for the test by studying.*)

prey (**pray**)

    noun an animal that is killed for food by another animal (*Rabbits are a common **prey** of wolves and foxes.*)

probability (prah buh **bih** luh tee)

    noun the chance or possibility that something will happen (*You can figure out the **probability** of an event using a special math formula.*)

process (**prah** ses)

    noun a series of events or actions that produce a result (*The **process** of turning salt water into fresh water is simple.*)

producer (pruh **doo** suhr)

   noun an organism that manufactures its own food and serves as food to other organisms (*The entire food chain is made up of* ***producers*** *and consumers.*)

propagate (**prah** puh gayt)

   verb to produce offspring (*Both plants and animals* ***propagate*** *and have offspring.*)

protein (**proh** teen)

   noun a substance that builds and keeps muscles healthy (***Proteins*** *are found in eggs, meats, and beans.*)

Rr

recessive (rih **seh** sihv)

   adjective weaker and less noticeable (*Although he had a* ***recessive*** *gene for blue eyes, his eyes were brown.*)

replication (**rep** li **kay** shuhn)

   noun a process in which cells make new cells (*Scientists can measure the rate of cell* ***replication*** *to find out many things about the human body.*)

reproduction (ree pruh **duk** shuhn)

   noun the process plants and animals use to create offspring (*We studied the* ***reproduction*** *of one-celled animals in biology class.*)

respiration (rehs puh **ray** shun)

   noun the process of breathing (*During* ***respiration***, *oxygen is provided to their blood.*)

respond (rih **spawnd**)

   verb to answer or react to something (*The teacher asked a question and called on me to* ***respond***.)

review (rih **vyoo**)

   verb to look over or study something again (*I* ***reviewed*** *all my notes when I was studying for the science test.*)

Ss

scavenger (**ska** vuhn juhr)

   noun an organism that feeds on dead animals that it has not killed (*A buzzard is a* ***scavenger***.)

segmentation (sehg muhn **tay** shun)

   noun the state of being divided into sections (*If you look closely at many worms, you can see the* ***segmentation***.)

selection (suh **lehk** shun)

   noun the act of choosing something (*Darwin believed in natural* ***selection***, *which is also known as "the survival of the fittest."*)

sensory (**sen** suh ree)

   adjective having to do with the five senses (*The human* ***sensory*** *system is made up of the senses of hearing, sight, smell, taste, and smell.*)

sequence (**see** kwuhns)

   noun a certain order of steps, events, numbers, or items (*The letters of the code followed a definite* ***sequence***.)

series (**sihr** eez)

   noun a number of things or events that come in a certain order (*The recipe followed a* ***series*** *of steps.*)

skeletal (**skeh** luh tuhl)

   adjective having to do with an animal's skeleton (*The* ***skeletal*** *system is the framework that supports the body.*)

specialize (**speh** shuh lyz)

   verb to do a specific job (*Nerve cells* ***specialize*** *in sending electronic pulses through the body.*)

species (**spee** sees)

   noun the lowest level of scientific classification (*Animals of the same* ***species*** *can reproduce.*)

spore (spohr)

noun a cell that some plants and fungi use to reproduce (*I stepped on a puffball in the woods and sent up a cloud of* **spores**.)

stimulus (stihm yuh lus)

noun something thatcauses a reaction (*The biology test on Tuesday was Bernie's* **stimulus** *to study all weekend.*)

summarize (suhm uh ryz)

verb to state the main points in a shortened way (*Esteban asked his teacher to* **summarize** *the lesson that he missed.*)

symbiosis (sihm bee **oh** suhs)

noun a close relationship between two organisms in which at least one is dependent on the other (*There is a* **symbiosis** *between the hippopotamus and the oxpecker bird that eats insects from the hippo's skin.*)

symmetry (sih muh tree)

noun having parts that balance or match one another (*The right and left sides of my face have* **symmetry**.)

Tt

taxonomy (tak **sah** nuh mee)

noun the classification of things, especially living organisms (*Scientific* **taxonomy** *has seven levels, beginning with kingdom and ending with species.*)

territorial (tehr uh **tawr** ee uhl)

adjective describes an animal that is protective of a certain area (*My dog is very* **territorial** *and barks whenever someone comes into our yard.*)

theory (thee uh ree)

noun a statement, based on facts, that explains why or how something happens (*Albert Einstein came up with the* **theory** *of relativity.*)

tissue (tih shoo)

noun a large group of cells in an animal or plant that are alike and do the same job (*After working out with weights, Darryl gained a lot of muscle* **tissue**.)

trait (trayt)

noun a feature or characteristic of the way something or someone acts or looks (*People respect others who demonstrate the* **traits** *of kindness and honesty.*)

transport (trans **pawrt**)

verb to move things (*The ions were* **transported** *through the membrane.*)

Vv

variable (vehr ee uh buhl)

noun the thing that is tested in an experiment (*The only* **variable** *in the experiment was the temperature of the water.*)

adjective able to change (*We had to allow for the* **variable** *weight of the packages.*)

variation (vehr ee **ay** shuhn)

noun a difference or change between two similar things (*There was a slight* **variation** *in the color of the two roses.*)

vascular (vas kyuh luhr)

adjective having to do with the system of veins and tubes in animals and plants that carry blood and other fluids (*The sap of a tree moves through its* **vascular** *system.*)

virus (vy ruhs)

noun a tiny organism that causes disease in plants and animals (*The common cold is caused by a* **virus** *that infects the mucous membranes in the nose and throat.*)